Life After Death?

Spiros Zodhiates

Life After Death?

AMG PUBLISHERS
CHATTANOOGA, TN 37422

Cover Design Marguerite Tittle
Illustrations Florence Anderson
Copyright 1977 by Spiros Zophiates
Printed in the United States of America
Second Printing 1987
Third Printing 1989
Fourth Printing 1994

1000-2-87

PREFACE

When you know something is going to happen, it's wise to prepare for it. If you're about to take a journey, you make sure your reservations are in order, that you have the proper clothing for the climate you're going to, and that nothing is left to chance.

Yet many people make no preparations for the most important journey of all, the one all of us must take from this life to the next. Face it; you're going to die someday unless the Lord Jesus Christ returns first. That's a real possibility, of course. But you need to be prepared for that eventuality, while not neglecting to prepare for the eventuality of death. Don't be afraid; God offers you the opportunity to acquire a faith that defies the fear of death.

However, don't believe the speculations of men about this subject. Eternity is too long to risk it on a guess. Only one person ever died and came back to tell us what happens after death. His name is Jesus Christ. Don't reject His testimony

on anyone's say-so. Be courageous enough to study and evaluate His life, and the evidences for His historicity. If He Himself is dependable, then the information He gives us is dependable also.

So many sects and false teachers have made varying pronouncements about the metaphysical state of man that I felt the necessity of a systematic study of the Scripture teaching from the original languages—especially from the Greek New Testament—so that there would be no doubt created by varying translations of the Bible.

This book was first written in the Greek language. The enthusiastic reception it has enjoyed among the Greek-speaking people of the world encouraged me to translate it into English, with a few variations necessary to adapt it to English-speaking readers. It is my hope that it will answer many of your questions as you study God's Word with its help.

This book is different from most of my other exegetical writings, in which I expounded chapters or books of the New Testament from the Greek text, giving the meaning of every important word. This is a treatise on a subject of extreme importance. My prayer is that the Holy Spirit will greatly use it.

Spiros Zodhiates

CONTENTS

I	WHERE ARE THE DEAD?	13
II	ERRORS CONCERNING MAN'S STATE AFTER DEATH	18
III	THE TWO ELEMENTS IN MAN'S NATURE	24
IV	IS OUR SPIRIT OR SOUL SIMPLY OUR BREATH?	30
V	WHAT IS DEATH?	36
VI	WHERE DO MEN'S DEPARTED SPIRITS GO? (PART 1)	42
VII	WHERE DO MEN'S DEPARTED SPIRITS GO? (PART 2)	49
VIII	WHERE IS SHEOL?	56
IX	INCORRUPTION, INCORRUPTIBILITY, IMMORTALITY	62
X	WHAT IS HADEES?	70
XI	DOES MAN BECOME "EXTINCT" AT DEATH? (PART 1)	79
XII	DOES MAN BECOME "EXTINCT" AT DEATH? (PART 2)	85
XIII	THE STATE OF THE SOUL AFTER DEATH (PART 1)	90
XIV	THE STATE OF THE SOUL AFTER DEATH (PART 2)	96
XV	WHAT IS PARADISE LIKE?	102
XVI	SHALL WE BE ABLE TO RECOGNIZE EACH OTHER IN PARADISE?	106
XVII	THE TWO RESURRECTIONS OF THE DEAD	111
XVIII	WHEN WILL THE RESURRECTION OF BELIEVERS TAKE PLACE? (PART 1)	116
XIX	WHEN WILL THE RESURRECTION OF BELIEVERS TAKE PLACE? (PART 2)	123
XX	THE RESURRECTION BODY, SIMILAR YET DIFFERENT	129

XXI   FURTHER PROOF THAT THE RIGH-
        TEOUS DEAD ARE IN HEAVEN   134
XXII   WHERE IS HEAVEN, AND WHO IS
        THERE?   141
XXIII   CHARACTERISTICS OF THE RESUR-
        RECTION BODY   145
XXIV   THE FINAL HEAVEN—WHAT IT WILL
        BE LIKE   151
XXV   THE PRESENT HELL (PART 1)   157
XXVI   THE PRESENT HELL (PART 2)   162
XXVII   THE THEORY OF THE RESTORATION
        OF ALL THINGS, OR SALVATION
        AFTER DEATH (PART 1)   171
XXVIII THE THEORY OF THE RESTORATION
        OF ALL THINGS, OR SALVATION
        AFTER DEATH (PART 2)   176
XXIX   THE THEORY OF THE RESTORATION
        OF ALL THINGS, OR SALVATION
        AFTER DEATH (PART 3)   185
XXX   WHAT THE BIBLE TEACHES ABOUT
        ETERNAL PUNISHMENT (PART 1)   193
XXXI   WHAT THE BIBLE TEACHES ABOUT
        ETERNAL PUNISHMENT (PART 2)   201
XXXII   WHAT IS MEANT BY CHRIST'S
        REGENERATION?   211
XXXIII THE CONSEQUENCES OF BELIEVING
        IN ULTIMATE UNIVERSAL SALVA-
        TION   215
XXXIV   THE ETERNAL HELL, GEHENNA, THE
        LAKE OF FIRE   222
XXXV   FURTHER SCRIPTURAL TEACHING
        ON THE STATE OF THE WICKED
        AFTER DEATH   228
XXXVI   WILL THE WICKED SUFFER ETER-
        NALLY?   238
XXXVII CAN ANYONE BE SURE OF HEAVEN?   245
XXXVIII HOW TO MAKE SURE YOU ARE GOING
        TO HEAVEN   251

Where Are the Dead?

"Here today and gone tomorrow." That's men's fatalistic
way of shrugging off the inevitability of death.
We know we can't escape it, yet we don't want to
think too deeply about it. But a number of questions continue to haunt us. Isn't it better to face
them now than to go on with a nagging uncer-
tainty forever at the back of our minds?

What are some of these uncertainties?
Perhaps most poignant of all is, where are our
loved ones who have gone on before? Is there
any possibility that we shall see them again? And
what about ourselves—what about you? Were
you born just to live for a number of years on this
earth and then disappear?

There are some groups of religious people,
notably the Jehovah's Witnesses, who would try
to persuade us that man goes to nothingness
when he dies. How can we know whether they are
right? What criteria can we use to judge?

First of all, we can't use human logic as a
criterion, because that applies only to the world

we live in. At best all it can offer us are conjectures about life beyond the grave. What it has to say on this matter would be purely hypothetical. And this question is far too vital to rest on mere guesswork. What we need is actual firsthand knowledge.

But is there anyone who possesses such knowledge? If there is, he would have to be someone who had lived, died, risen again, and had come back to tell us the answer to this mystery. Is there such a person? Yes, indeed. He is Jesus Christ. And how do we know we can rely on what He has to say? Because His life was completely different from that of any other man—it was miraculous and attested by miracles.

Have you ever seen a young person lying dead in a coffin and, as he was being carried to the cemetery, brought back to life by the touch of a bystander? Christ did just that. He also commanded a dead man, Lazarus, to come out of the tomb, and Lazarus did. Christ walked on the waters of the Sea of Galilee. He fed thousands of men, women, and children with a few fishes and a little bread. He touched the eyes of the blind and restored their sight. He made the lame walk, the deaf hear, and the lepers clean. He did what was humanly impossible.

"But He died," you say. True, but not out of necessity, as you and I and all men must die. He died of His own volition. What other man could say to his potential executioner: "No man taketh it [my life] from me, but I lay it down of myself. I have power to lay it down, and I have power to take it again" (John 10:18)? Pilate ordered that Christ be nailed to the cross. But he could do it only because Christ gave him the authority to do it. Pilate may have thought he was acting as a free agent in ordering Christ to be crucified. What he didn't know was that he was able to do this only because God had allowed it in His divine wisdom and plan.

How can we prove this? Christ Himself proved it when He rose from the dead, just as He had predicted before the event. Show me another person who has done that and I'll be prepared to believe whatever he has to tell me about matters I myself am unable to investigate. Christ alone has the right to reveal these things to us. You can believe Him or not. But who will be the loser if you don't? Certainly not Christ, but you. The decision is now up to you.

There is another criterion by which we can judge these matters. It is the Sacred Scriptures. Christ is the fulfillment of the Old Testament. Through His resurrection He placed His seal upon it, giving it absolute authority as God's infallible Word. It is on this Scriptural basis that we shall find out what He has revealed to us about what happens after death.

Can science shed any light on the problem? We live in an age that has practically deified science. But what can scientists tell us about a father or mother or loved child who has gone before? What consolation or assurance can a scientist give us on the basis of science alone that we will see our loved ones again? Science of itself stands mute in the presence of dead bodies.

Of course, bio-chemical science can tell us what happens to the body. We know that a dead body is dissolved into its component elements. Yet, though its present construction and form disappear, it is not annihilated. Its matter is converted into other forms.

If we weigh a man just before he dies and immediately afterward, there will be no ascertainable difference in weight. Yet something is gone. He has lost what constituted his vitality, the very thing that gave meaning and identity to his body. This aspect has no physical weight, yet it is the one that really effects the difference between life and death. This is what we call a man's soul or spirit. When someone dies, we say he "gave up the ghost," an archaic expression meaning his spirit has departed. Where does this immaterial man go? Does he disappear forever? Is he annihilated, or does he continue to exist in another form, quite different from the body that he abandoned on earth?

Only Scripture can give us authoritative answers regarding the habitation of the soul or spirit after death. Scripture reveals the beginning, the nature, and the final destination of man. Have you ever seriously searched the Scriptures

16

to find out who you are, where you came from, where you're going, what the meaning of life and death is, and what happens after death?

Some people, knowingly or unknowingly, are promulgating unscriptural answers to these questions. Don't let preconceptions or prejudices turn you off at this point. Be honest enough to examine the proofs set forth here and evaluate them in the light of the whole teaching of Scripture.

Errors concerning Man's State after Death

The Jehovah's Witnesses, whose first leaders were two Americans, "Pastor" Charles Taze Russell and Judge J. F. Rutherford, have filled the world with their books, published in many languages. Their aim seems to be, not to lead men to Christ and the salvation He offers, but to win them to their distinctively different doctrines.

One of these doctrines refers to man's state after death. It teaches that man is annihilated at the moment of death, that is, he loses conscious existence until the day of final resurrection. Another of their controversial doctrines is that there is no such state as hell, and that all the faithless dead will have a second chance to be saved.

They claim the authority of the Holy Scriptures in support of their erroneous doctrines. However, they handle the Scriptures in a most irresponsible and illogical manner, repressing many passages, misinterpreting others, and taking others out of context. This is actually the way to heresy—*haeresis* in Greek, which signifies "private opinion, as opposed to knowledge of the truth." Any opinion is heretical that fails to conform to the truth as it is revealed by God in the whole context of the Scriptures.

This is the condemnation under which the exegetical methods of the Jehovah's Witnesses falls. They interpret many verses in isolation, apart from their context—a method by which anyone can "prove" almost anything. As the old rhyme goes,

Of all the arts sagacious dupes invent,

The worst is Scripture warped from its intent!

As an example of this, we might quote four words from Psalm 14:1, "There is no God." But if we look up this verse, the false conclusion we have arrived at will immediately become apparent, for the whole verse reads, "The fool hath said in his heart, There is no God"—a quite different matter.

In order to understand any verse, passage, or quotation from Scripture, we need to know who said it, under what circumstances, and whether or not the whole teaching of Scripture is in agreement or disagreement with it. If the meaning is not obvious, and this may often be the case, we must examine parallel passages in Scripture to shed light on the particular meaning intended.

Thus we need to search the Scriptures and

study them carefully, praying at the same time that the Spirit of God who inspired their authors to write them may guide us to the whole truth. It is not enough to be able to quote Scripture in support of our views. We must be acquainted with the "mind" of the Scriptures to be able to discern their true intent, so that we may quote them correctly in support or refutation of any controversial doctrine. The Holy Scriptures are the source of truth, and we must handle them honestly, with the intention of converting our minds to the truth contained in them, rather than of supporting our own philosophical theories or man-made theological systems.

What we have stated here constitutes the test of theological objectivity—not coming to the Scriptures to find verses that will buttress our own previously formed opinions, but to find the revealed truth of God in the Bible as a whole, so that we may know the mind of God on any given matter. God's revealed Word to man makes man truly rational and intellectually free.

The Jehovah's Witnesses have failed this test because they hold fast to their own subjective theories by wresting Scripture from its clear intent. Instead of freedom they fall prey to psychosis and mental delusion. The only way they can be delivered is through a patient and loving expose of the errors they have been led into, and by telling them the truth as it is made evident in God's Word—praying that the Holy Spirit will bring them under genuine conviction and conversion.

The basic teachings of the Jehovah's Witnesses are contained in the six volumes of "Pastor" Russell's *Studies in the Scriptures.* These volumes were accepted *in toto* by Rutherford, Russell's successor, and ever since by the vast majority of Jehovah's Witnesses. In these volumes we find their beliefs about life after death.

In the first place, they hold that no man has a soul. They claim that the teachers of Christendom, that is, the whole Christian world, including Protestants, Roman Catholics, and Eastern Orthodox, have persuaded the world in general to believe that man carries within himself a living soul that flies away after death to some other abode. Through the use of such disparaging terminology they not only express their disagreement with Christian doctrine but also seek to ridicule and condemn all of Christendom.

Russell defines death as a period of absolute annihilation. Judge Rutherford says that sinners have no conscious existence when they are placed in the grave. Consequently they do not suffer, simply because they do not exist. He also claims that the sinner who dies is not conscious of himself, and he would have remained in this unconscious state or state of non-existence forever had God not made some provision for his restoration. By this "provision" he means the resurrection and the so-called second chance.

Regarding the resurrection, the second chance, and hell, the Jehovah's Witnesses believe that those who die will one day be raised in a state of spiritual existence. They teach that the Apostles and all true 'Christians' who died before 1878 arose in the spring of that year as incorporeal spiritual beings. They also teach that the unrighteous dead will one day arise and be given a second chance to believe in God and thus find their salvation. This concerns the period of a thousand years, or their doctrine of Chiliasm. This name is used because it derives from the Greek word *chilieteeris,* meaning "a thousand years." Russell says that things will be more opportune during this period, and the work of Christ will avail for this second time. In other words, we may presume that even Nero, Hitler, and all others of that ilk will have a chance to be saved, provided they reject their past behavior and obey Jesus' call.

The Jehovah's Witnesses deny that there will be any eternal punishment other than annihilation. God is good and therefore He cannot and will not tolerate eternal torment in hell. The punishment of those who will not believe and obey Jesus during this period of the second chance, and therefore will not receive salvation and life, will be a second death resulting in eternal annihilation of being.

These, in brief, are the teachings of Russell

and Rutherford about the life beyond. What follows in the next chapters of this book is the presentation of evidence to show that man is not annihilated after death, that he exists in a conscious state, and that there is no second chance for salvation after the resurrection. Our arguments will be based entirely on the Sacred Scriptures, the only authoritative and convincing source of truth, following the methods of objective analysis set forth in the beginning of this chapter.

The Two Elements
in Man's Nature

Scripture teaches that man is made up of two elements, the physical and the spiritual. These are clearly distinguished from one another, though they appear together and in fact constitute a unity.

We have pointed out Russell and Rutherford's teaching, that man does not possess a soul, that he has no spiritual constituent that is not dependent on the human body for its continued existence. Here, however, is some Scriptural evidence that directly contradicts these contentions and definitely proves that man's nature includes a spiritual element quite distinct from his material body.

Job 32:8: "But there is a spirit in man: and the inspiration of the Almighty giveth them understanding."

Zechariah 12:1: "The burden of the word of the Lord for Israel, saith the Lord, which stretcheth forth the heavens, and layeth the foundation of the earth, and formeth the spirit of man within him."

These verses clearly distinguish between the spirit that is in man and the whole man, in the same way that a house is distinguished from its occupant.

Job 14:22: "But his flesh upon him shall have pain, and his soul within him shall mourn." Here we have a distinction between flesh and soul. The flesh is presented as the external cover of the soul, which constitutes the internal part of man's nature.

I Corinthians 6:20: "For ye are bought with a price: therefore glorify God in your body, and in your spirit, which are God's." The distinction between body and soul here is unquestionable.

I Corinthians 2:11: "For what man knoweth the things of a man, save the spirit of man which is in him? even so the things of God knoweth no man, but the Spirit of God." This verse proves again that man has within him a spiritual element quite distinct from his body, an element that enables him to think and understand.

Man's spiritual element is further discernible in the Lord's teaching as seen in Matthew 10:28: "And fear not them which kill the body, but are not able to kill the soul: but rather fear him which is able to destroy both soul and body in hell."

The body, then, is conclusively shown not to be identical with the soul, or the soul with the body. If they were one and the same, the death of one would at the same time entail the death of the other. But though this is what the Jehovah's Witnesses claim, it is in sharp contrast to our Lord's statement in Matthew 10:28.

It is important in this connection to have a look at the creation of man. God created him with a composite nature, both material and spiritual. This can readily be seen in the creation narratives of Genesis 1 and 2. Genesis 2:7 is especially important in support of this view: "And the Lord God formed man of the dust of the ground, and breathed into his nostrils the breath of life; and man became a living soul."

This verse makes clear the precise order that God followed in creating man. He first shaped man from the common clay of earth. That was his body, the material element of his existence. Yet at this point, though the body was complete in every detail, it was motionless and lifeless. "Life," that element which makes the heart beat and the mind think, was not there. Neither was there any self-consciousness or feeling. There was only a body, the product of God's first creative act on behalf of man.

Then God took a second step. He "breathed into his nostrils the breath of life; and man became a living soul." In this way God gave man a spiritual element within the outward casing of his body. In contrast to the body, the spiritual element was an immaterial one; it was the element that would make the body live and move. It was because of this that "man became a living soul."

The expression, "a living soul," does not imply that the material and spiritual elements were unified in such a way that they could not be distinguished. Such a view would contradict all the verses we have already referred to, and many others that clearly distinguish between these two elements. Consequently we are to understand the expression, "a living soul," as implying that the life of man is based on the spirit that God breathed into his body in the second step of His creative action. The body, then, is not alive of itself, but only in and through the soul. It is the soul that enables it to move, eat, drink, act, and in one word *live*. It is because the soul occupies this basic place and plays such a vital role in the life of man that it is used to describe or denote the whole man. We say, for example, "There are 40 souls in this room" but we never say, "There are 40 bodies in this room." The body cannot be conceived of without a soul, while the soul, when reference is made to man's earthly existence, is always embodied.

We see, therefore, that the Jehovah's Witnesses are in error when they say that man *has* no soul because he himself *is* a soul. Man is a soul that lives in a body and constitutes the life-giving principle of that body. The body is not identical with the soul nor the soul with the body. If they were identical, the Lord would never have said that the body could be killed, but the soul could not be killed (Matthew 10:28).

Scripture not only distinguishes between the material and spiritual elements that constitute man; it also introduces another distinction within the spiritual element. The Apostle Paul distinguishes between man's soul and his spirit, thus giving us to understand that there are two elements that constitute the immaterial part of man. "And the very God of peace sanctify you wholly; and I pray God your whole spirit and soul and body be preserved blameless unto the coming of our Lord Jesus Christ" (I Thess. 5:23). A similar distinction is apparent in Hebrews 4:12: "For the word of God is quick, and powerful, and sharper than any twoedged sword, piercing even to the dividing asunder of soul and spirit, and of the joints and marrow, and is a discerner of the thoughts and intents of the heart." We see here that man is composed of three elements: body, soul, and spirit.

It is significant to note, then, that man was created in the image and likeness of God (Gen. 1:26, 27), and that God is triune—although this is another Scriptural truth that the Jehovah's Witnesses deny. "And God said, Let us make man in *our* image, after *our* likeness." Note the plural pronouns, instead of the singular *my*. Since God is triune, man made in His image is also triune.

We shall not enlarge here, however, on the distinction between soul and spirit. Our purpose so far has been to prove that Scripture teaches

28

that man has a spiritual element pervading his body that is composed of soul and spirit. Sometimes these two terms are used as being synonymous in Scripture, but whether used synonymously or distinctively they both refer to the spiritual element in man. This is important and should always be kept in mind when we use these two terms.

Here, perhaps, we should refer to a point that relates to the spirit. This is that aspect of man's immaterial nature that enables him to communicate with God, who is also Spirit. "But the natural man receiveth not the things of the Spirit of God: for they are foolishness unto him: neither can he know them, because they are spiritually discerned." The spirit is the window in man's immaterial nature that allows him to perceive God. The soul is that aspect of his immaterial nature that makes him aware of his body and his natural, physical environment. The difference between soul and spirit is not one of substance but of operation.

Thus we must say that man's immaterial aspect is represented in Scripture by the single terms "spirit" or "soul," or both of them together. (See Gen. 35:18; 41:8, I Kings 17:21, Ps. 42:6, Prov. 20:27, Eccles. 12:7, Matt. 10:28; 20:28; 27:50, Mark 8:36, 37; 12:30, Luke 1:46, John 12:27; 13:21, I Cor. 2:14; 5:3; 15:44, Eph. 4:23, I Thess. 5:23, Heb. 4:12; 6:18, 19; 12:23, James 1:21; 2:26, III John 2, Rev. 6:9; 20:4.)

Is Our Spirit or Soul Simply Our Breath?

One of the greater errors of the Jehovah's Witnesses is the contention that whenever the term "spirit" is used, as for example "the spirit which is in man," it signifies "breath." They also claim that in death man's breath (spirit) disappears and is in fact annihilated.

Is this Scriptural? Let us examine whether the words "spirit" and "breath," when referring to the inner element of man which vivifies him, are synonymous. In Job 34:14, 15 we read: "If he set his heart upon man, if he gather unto himself his spirit and his breath; all flesh shall perish together, and man shall turn again unto dust." Here it is evident that spirit and breath refer to two distinct things. If we were to suppose them synonymous, the verse would read: "If he set his heart upon man, if he gather unto himself his spirit and his spirit [or his breath and his breath]." Spirit and breath are not always synonymous in Scripture. If they were, we would be able to substitute the word "breath" for "spirit" in the following verses. Let's try it and see whether it makes sense:

Acts 23:8: "For the Sadducees say that there is no resurrection, neither angel, nor *breath:* but the Pharisees confess both."

Acts 23:9: "And there arose a great cry: and the scribes that were of the Pharisees' part arose, and strove, saying, We find no evil in this man: but if a *breath* or an angel hath spoken to him, let us not fight against God."

Romans 2:29: "But he is a Jew, which is one inwardly; and circumcision is that of the heart, in the *breath,* and not in the letter; whose praise is not of men, but of God."

I Corinthians 5:5: "To deliver such an one unto Satan for the destruction of the flesh, that the *breath* may be saved in the day of the Lord Jesus."

II Corinthians 7:1: "Having therefore these promises, dearly beloved, let us cleanse ourselves from all filthiness of the flesh and *breath,* perfecting holiness in the fear of God."

Galatians 6:18: "Brethren, the grace of our Lord Jesus Christ be with your *breath.* Amen."

Similarly, let us try substituting the word "breath" for "soul" to prove how illogical is the contention that the spirit or soul of man is nothing but his breath.

Psalm 19:7: "The law of the Lord is perfect, converting the *breath.*"

Matthew 10:18: "And fear not them which

31

kill the body, but are not able to kill the *breath:* but rather fear him which is able to destroy both *breath* and body in hell.''

Luke 12:19: "And I will say to my *breath, Breath,* thou hast much goods laid up for many years; take thine ease, eat, drink, and be merry.''

I Thessalonians 5:23: "And the very God of peace sanctify you wholly; and I pray God your whole spirit and *breath* and body be preserved blameless unto the coming of our Lord Jesus Christ.''

James 5:20: "Let him know, that he which converteth the sinner from the error of his way, shall save a *breath* from death, and shall hide a multitude of sins.''

II Peter 2:8: "(For that righteous man dwelling among them, in seeing and hearing, vexed his righteous *breath* from day to day with their unlawful deeds.)''

These substitutions show how impossible are the claims of the Jehovah's Witnesses that the soul and spirit signify the breath of man. Don't forget the verses we examined in chapter 3 to prove that man is not simply composed of a material element but also of an immaterial, spiritual one. You can search the Scriptures for yourself and discover numerous other examples.

Think about this: our bodies are constantly changing. From a material point of view we are not the same persons today as we were seven years ago. Biological science tells us that over the course of seven years our old cells have been completely replaced by new ones, that in fact we possess a new physical body and even new physical brains. And this happens every seven years.

Yet, though our brains change every seven years, we still remember things we learned much longer ago than that. This clearly indicates that there is something inside our constantly changing bodies that always remains indestructible. This is yet another clear indication that man possesses a spirit that constitutes his real indwelling self. It is clearly distinguished from the body, and Scripture teaches that it continues to live even after the dissolution of the body. How else can we explain Paul's desire "to be absent from the body, and to be present with the Lord" (II Cor. 5:8)?

These observations are in absolute agreement with Paul's statement in I Corinthians 2:11: "For what man knoweth the things of a man, save the spirit of man which is in him? even so the things of God knoweth no man, but the Spirit of God." How is it possible for the Jehovah's Witnesses to deny the existence of the spirit in man and yet continue to claim that they base their contentions on the Scriptures?

The center of human knowledge is not basically the gray matter that makes up the human brain. If it were so, we would be able to analyze this substance and create similar brains capable of thinking, remembering, loving, hating, and deciding. We do have mechanical brains, electronically controlled, but these are dependent on man to activate and maintain them. They cannot set themselves in motion, working instantaneously as self-activated machines, as our brains do. Our brains work this way because there is something other than material in us that thinks, senses, and decides. This something cannot be explained by scientific observations and theories; nevertheless all men are conscious of its operations and products.

When our physical element is asleep, we all know that our immaterial nature, our mind, or spirit, or soul, whatever name we give it, continues to function—to dream, to deal with problems, to remember past events. It follows, then that it is not the material or physical brain that makes man think and decide and act, but the immaterial mind that pervades each one of us. This is our spirit, that immaterial aspect of our nature by which we can communicate with God.

When man's body dies, his physical brains, eyes, ears, nerves, etc., continue for a while to be the same parts of the body that they were before death; but the brain cannot think, the eyes cannot see, the ears cannot hear, and the nerves cannot sense. Why is this? Because it was not his material body but his spiritual element that enabled him to think, see, hear, and sense.

Dr. William Mayo, famous surgeon and founder of the world-renowned Mayo Clinic, said: "This elegant penknife of mine may never discover the soul, this mysterious side of man. However I know that it is there. I am as certain that there is a soul in man as I am of the most basic principles of my medical science."

What Is Death?

Death is the separation of the two basic elements of man's nature, the immaterial from the material, the spirit or soul from the body.

We have seen that man was created by God with a material body and a non-material soul. When man ceases to exist as a union of spirit or soul with body, we say he is dead. Life is the union of soul and body. Death is the disassociation of the two. Again let us show the truth of this from the Scriptures.

The Bible reveals that death came upon man as God's curse, just as life was granted to him as God's gift. In Genesis 3:19 we read God's sentence on Adam: "In the sweat of thy face shalt thou eat bread, till thou return unto the ground; for out of it wast thou taken: for dust thou art, and unto dust shalt thou return." This verse refers to man's body, for only the body was taken from the earth according to the Genesis narrative, and it is this alone that goes back to the earth. The breath of life (Gen. 2:7), that spirit or soul that God breathed into man's body, was neither earthly nor taken from the earth. Therefore, since its origin was not from the earth, neither is its destiny to return to the earth. In every instance where Scripture refers to death as the end of man's life on earth, it is the death of the body that is spoken of, and not the soul. Whenever the soul is mentioned in connection with death, it means its separation from the body. Consider these revealing verses:

Ecclesiastes 8:8: "There is no man that hath power over the spirit to retain the spirit; neither hath he power in the day of death: and there is no discharge in that war; neither shall wickedness deliver those that are given to it."

Ecclesiastes 12:7: "Then shall the dust return to the earth as it was: and the spirit shall return unto God who gave it."

It is obvious that this latter verse refers to Genesis 3:19, "For dust thou art, and unto dust shalt thou return." God meant by this the body of man only; and Ecclesiastes 12:7 makes it plain that the spirit returns unto God who gave it.

In Scripture death is often synonymous with the delivering up of the spirit. In these passages, the word "ghost" and "spirit" are synonymous. Thus we read that Abraham "gave up the ghost, and died" (Gen. 25:8), and "Isaac gave up the ghost, and died" (Gen. 35:29), and Jacob "yielded up the ghost, and was gathered unto his people" (Gen. 49:33). Note that Scripture says he "was gathered unto his people," not that he disappeared. Why then do the Jehovah's Witnesses assert that death is annihilation?

Now note what Scripture says about Christ's death. "And when Jesus had cried with a loud voice, he said, Father, into thy hands I commend my spirit: and having said thus, he gave up the ghost" (Luke 23:46).

Job 14:10 tells us, "But man dieth, and wasteth away: yea, man giveth up the ghost, and where is he?"

In Acts 5:10 we read: "Then fell she [Sapphira] down straightway at his feet, and yielded up the ghost: and the young men came in, and found her dead, and carrying her forth, buried her by her husband."

Throughout Scripture, the yielding up of the spirit or the giving up the spirit means death. The inescapable conclusion is that death is the separation of the spirit or soul from the body.

I Kings 17:20-22 makes this very clear. It tells of the prophet Elijah praying for the resurrection of the widow's son at Zarephath. "And he cried unto the Lord, and said, O Lord my God, hast thou also brought evil upon the widow with whom I sojourn, by slaying her son? And he stretched himself upon the child three times, and cried unto the Lord, and said, O Lord my God, I pray thee, let this child's soul come into him again. And the Lord heard the voice of Elijah; and the soul of the child came into him again, and he revived." Here it is obvious that the child's soul departed from his body when the child died, and came back into it when he lived again.

In the Gospel of Luke we find a similar case. The daughter of the ruler of the synagogue had died. By what means was her revival effected? By the power of Jesus Christ. And how is this expressed? Luke 8:55 tells us, "And her spirit came again, and she arose straightway . . . ." Death occurred when her spirit abandoned her body; life was restored when her spirit came back.

When David heard that his beloved child had died (II Sam. 12:19-23), he stopped weeping and fasting. When asked why he reacted in that way, he replied, "But now he is dead, wherefore should I fast? can I bring him back again? I shall go to him, but he shall not return to me" (v. 23). Thus we see that though David knew his child could not return to earth, he expected that one day he would go to meet his son.

Paul also declares that death is the separation of spirit and body. In II Corinthians 5:6-9 he says, "Therefore we are always confident, knowing that, whilst we are at home in the body, we are absent from the Lord: (for we walk by faith, not by sight:) We are confident, I say, and willing rather to be absent from the body, and to be present with the Lord. Wherefore we labour, that, whether present or absent, we may be accepted of him." What does he mean by saying, "we are at home in the body" and "to be absent from the body"? Without doubt he strongly implies that the soul or spirit are distinguished from the body and are separated from it at death. During this life the soul is at home in the body, and at death it leaves the body. No other logical explanation can be deduced from these verses.

Paul symbolically refers to the body as a tent or tabernacle which is indwelt by our spiritual or real self. "For we know that if our earthly house of this tabernacle were dissolved, we have a building of God, an house not made with hands, eternal in the heavens" (II Cor. 5:1).

Peter uses the same symbolism. "Yea, I think it meet, as long as I am in this tabernacle, to stir you up by putting you in remembrance; knowing that shortly I must put off this my tabernacle, even as our Lord Jesus Christ hath shewed me. Moreover I will endeavour that ye may be able after my decease to have these things always in remembrance" (II Pet. 1:13-15).

The body, then, is the tabernacle that man leaves at death, but he himself continues to exist as a self-conscious though immaterial entity.

That the faithful Christian is not annihilated at death, but departs to be with the Lord while he abandons his body, is clearly evident in what Paul wrote to the Philippians: "For to me to live is Christ, and to die is gain. But if I live in the flesh, this is the fruit of my labour: yet what I shall choose I wot not. For I am in a strait betwixt two, having a desire to depart, and to be with Christ;

which is far better: nevertheless to abide in the flesh is more needful for you" (Phil. 1:21-24).

That death means separation of the spirit from the body is further apparent from the following verses:

II Timothy 4:6: "For I am now ready to be offered, and the time of my departure is at hand."

Genesis 35:18: "And it came to pass, as her soul was in departing, (for she died) . . . ."

Luke 2:29: "Lord, now lettest thou thy servant depart in peace, according to thy word."

James 2:26: "For as the body without the spirit is dead, so faith without works is dead also."

Remember, if you cannot substitute the word "breath" for soul and spirit in the verses mentioned in chapter 4, you cannot arbitrarily do so here.

Where Do Men's Departed Spirits Go? (Part 1)

We have shown from the Scriptures that death means the separation or departure of the spirit or soul of man from his body. Now let us see what the Bible has to say about where these departed spirits go. God's Word is our only certified revelation. It has been certified and verified by the risen Christ. If Christ had not constantly spoken "according to the Scriptures" and had not connected His person with the Scriptures, we would have no reliable source of information today. Whatever else is said or claimed on this subject, apart from Scripture, is mere sophistry or human myth.

We begin with Christ's own words as recorded in Luke 16:22, 23: "And it came to pass, that the beggar died, and was carried by the angels into Abraham's bosom: the rich man also died, and was buried; and in hell he lift up his eyes, being in torments, and seeth Abraham afar off, and Lazarus in his bosom." "Abraham's bosom" and "hell," these are the two names attributed here to the dwellings of departed spirits in the world to come. There are other terms that refer to these places.

Gehenna (Matt. 23:33): "Ye serpents, Ye generation of vipers, how can ye escape the damnation of hell *[gehenna* in the Greek text]."

Tartaros (II Pet. 2:4): "For if God spared not the angels that sinned, but cast them down to hell *[tartaros,* or the participle *tartarosas* in the Greek text], and delivered them into chains of darkness, to be reserved unto judgment."

Now let's turn to the Old Testament to see what terms are used to describe or name the habitation of the spirits of the dead.

In Genesis 37:35, Jacob, who believed that Joseph had been killed by a wild animal, declared, "I will go down into the grave unto my son mourning." The translation of the Hebrew word *sheol* here as "grave" is erroneous.

Psalm 16:10: "For thou wilt not leave my soul in hell"—again *sheol,* which here is more accurately translated "hell." It is not possible for one and the same Hebrew word to mean both "grave" and "hell," for in the Greek language we shall see in detail that "grave" and "hell" are two different things.

Numbers 16:30: "But if the Lord make a new thing, and the earth open her mouth, and swallow them up, with all that appertain unto them, and they go down quick into the pit; then ye shall understand that these men have provoked the Lord." Here the text refers to the situation of the unrighteous after death. The Hebrew word translated "pit" here is again *sheol.* It is clear that the term *sheol* is used in the Old Testament as synonymous with the term "hell" in the New Testament, to signify the place where the departed spirits of the dead dwell.

The word *sheol* is used 65 times in the Old Testament. To prove that *sheol* and hell are synonymous, it is sufficient to compare Psalm 16:10 with Acts 2:27, the latter being a quotation of the former in the New Testament, referring to the Messiah. The text in Acts reads as follows: "Because thou wilt not leave my soul in hell, neither wilt thou suffer thine Holy One to see corruption." The Hebrew text of Psalm 16:10 uses the word *sheol* instead of the word hell.

In the Greek Old Testament, known as the Septuagint Version, the work *sheol* is always translated by the word hell. *Sheol,* then, or hell, is the abode of the spirits or souls of the dead.

Rutherford and his followers contend that *sheol* or hell is simply the grave, the piece of land within which we place the bodies of the dead. We shall show that this contention is manifestly groundless.

The Hebrew word for grave is *qeber;* the Greek word is *mneemeion.* They are both widely used in the Scriptures. Now note that the words *sheol* and hell are never used in their plural form. But the word *qeber* appears in the plural 27 times, as *qeberim.* And *mneemeion* occurs in the plural as *mneemeia.* It follows then that the word *sheol* or hell signifies one place only, while the words *qeber* and *mneemeion* are used to signify many places. It is never said, "This is my own *sheol* or hell," but it is often said, "This is my own *mneemeion* or *qeber.*" The *qeber* or *mneemeion* is used exclusively for one person, but this is not so with *sheol* or hell, which is used in a general sense.

In Genesis 50:5 we read: "My father made me swear, saying, Lo, I die: in my grave which I have digged for me in the land of Canaan, there shalt thou bury me." Graves are said to belong to various persons (Num. 19:16, II Sam. 3:32, I Kings 13:30, II Chron. 34:28, Jer. 8:1, etc.). *Sheol* and hell are never said to belong to any particular person or even to some persons.

Furthermore, the body is never said to exist in hell, nor is it ever said that the spirit dwells in the grave. The grave is for the body, and hell or *sheol* is for the spirit. It is never said that a sheol was dug in the ground and a spirit deposited there. But it is often said that graves were dug in the ground. (Cf. Gen. 50:13, Exod. 14:11, II Sam. 21:14, Neh. 2:5, Ezek. 39:11.)

The *qeber* or *mneemeion* is used to indicate the site where the body is placed. "And he laid his carcase [body] in his own grave" (I Kings 13:30; see also II Kings 13:21, Ps. 88:5, Jer. 26:23). *Sheol* is never used in relation to the body; it is related only to the soul or spirit of man.

45

Qeber is used in relation to a place or space on the earth, in the same way as other possessions like buildings, fields, etc. (See Gen. 23:4, 9, 20.) *Sheol,* however, is never mentioned as someone's possession. *Qeber* is dug in the ground, and therefore is a material or physical entity. "Lo, I die: in my grave which I have digged for me in the land of Canaan, there shalt thou bury me" (Gen. 50:5, cf. Neh. 2:5). *Sheol* is never said to have been dug or excavated.

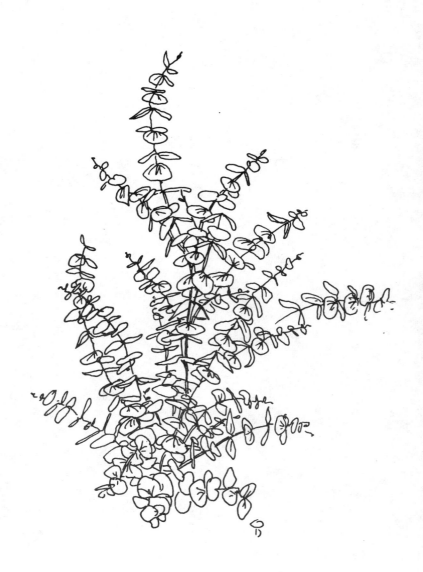

Where Do Men's Departed Spirits Go? (Part 2)

Continuing our study of what happens to the spirit of man when his body dies, there is one instance in the Scriptures that we should refer to, in case our readers think we have left it out on purpose. It is the occasion of the revolt of Korah, Dathan, and Abiram against Moses, in the 16th chapter of Numbers. Moses, desirous of proving that the Lord was with him, prophesied that these rebels would not die in a way that was common to all men. "But if the Lord make a new thing, and the earth open her mouth, and swallow them up, with all that appertain unto them, and they go down quick into the pit; then ye shall understand that these men have provoked the Lord" (v. 30). Moses predicted that the earth would open her "mouth" and swallow them up. In this way they would be killed and buried simultaneously. This prophecy was fulfilled. It entailed their physical death. But what happened to their real self, that is, their spirit? "They go down quick into the pit [sheol]." This phrase tells us that at the moment of their physical death their souls would depart to hell, where they would meet their punishment. It was not their bodies, then, that went down into hell but their spirits. They went down to hell at the very moment (simultaneously) that their bodies were buried in the earth. Clearly, then, this verse in no way indicates that hell and the grave are one and the same place.

For the unrighteous, *sheol* means pain and sorrow. Deuteronomy 32:22 says, "For a fire is kindled in mine anger, and shall burn unto the lowest hell, and shall consume the earth with her increase, and set on fire the foundations of the mountains." And in II Samuel 22:6 we read: "The sorrows of hell compassed me about; the snares of death prevented me." Psalm 116:3 says, "The sorrows of death compassed me, and the pains of hell gat hold upon me: I found trouble and sorrow."

But the word *qeber* is never used in connection with judgment or punishment. The body laid in the grave is senseless. It cannot taste pain or sorrow. It is the soul or spirit that has departed to *sheol* that senses and understands.

Sheol is always connected with the soul, never with the body. Psalm 16:10 declares, "For thou wilt not leave my soul [not the body] in hell." And in Psalm 86:13 we read, "Thou hast delivered my soul from the lowest hell."

Qeber, then, is never used in relation to the soul but to the body.

Sheol is also used in connection with the cry of desolation. Jonah 2:2 tells us, "I cried by reason of mine affliction unto the Lord, and he heard me; out of the belly of hell cried I, and thou heardest my voice." Jonah here compares his being in the belly of the great fish to being in *sheol,* along with its sufferings.

Qeber, the grave, cannot voice the plea or cry of one who is abandoned and confused, for a dead body can neither sense nor cry.

Sheol is connected with the thought that we go down into it. "For I will go down into the grave *[sheol]* unto my son mourning" (Gen. 37:35). Here the word *sheol* was erroneously translated "grave." The correct rendering is "hell." These are the words of Jacob when he received the false report that a wild beast had killed his son Joseph.

The thought that men go down to *sheol* is expressed in many other verses. It has a metaphorical meaning that relates to the judgment of God in death. That Jacob did not mean the physical grave of his son is clearly seen in the actual story. He believed that Joseph had been eaten by some wild beast, so that he couldn't possibly have been buried. That is why he didn't ask to see Joseph's grave, but looked forward to the time when he should go down to *sheol* and meet him there. A dead body cannot meet another dead body. Only the spirit of a dead person can meet and consciously communicate with

51

the spirit of another dead person. What good would it do Jacob if his dead body were to be buried in the same place as Joseph's?

When loved ones die, we often hear the bereaved say, "I want to go to be with him, too." Do they mean that they want their body to be buried in the same grave, or that they desire their spirit to depart to be in the same place as the spirit of the one they have lost?

A similar thought was expressed when Samuel said to Saul, "And to morrow shalt thou and thy sons be with me" (I Sam. 28:19). What he implied was not the grave, for Samuel well knew that soldiers killed on the battlefield were not always buried. As for Saul's body, the Philistines didn't find it until the next day, or two days after his talk with Samuel. They severed his head from his body, and fastened the body itself to the wall of Beth-shan. Some time elapsed before the people of Jabesh-gilead heard of what the Philistines had done to Saul. They traveled all night, found the bodies of Saul and his sons, and brought them back to Jabesh, where they burnt them.

As for Samuel, he was buried in Rama, while the bones of Saul and his sons were buried in Jabesh. It is obvious, then, that Samuel did not mean the grave when he said, "Tomorrow shalt thou and thy sons be with me."

Samuel knew that the soul survives after death. He knew the exact meaning of *sheol*. He knew that Saul would go where he was, and that all men go there when they die.

Jacob's death also is instructive as showing clearly that hell, or the place of the departed spirits of the dead, is not the same as the grave. We read in Genesis 49:33 that Jacob "yielded up the ghost, and was gathered unto his people." This "gathering" or "addition" refers to his soul or spirit at the moment of his death. It could not possibly refer to his body, because his dead body was embalmed and not buried until many months later. Jacob died in Egypt, but he was buried in Canaan. Forty days were required for embalming, and thirty more days were required for mourning. That brings us to seventy days after the death of Jacob. Then Joseph obtained permission from Pharoah to go to Canaan to bury his father (see Gen. 50:3-6). The Scripture narrative does not record how long it took Joseph to make this journey. It tells us that the funeral party mourned for seven more days at the threshingfloor of Atad beyond the Jordan (Gen. 50:10). It is certain that it was at least eighty days from the day when Jacob "was gathered unto his people" in death to the day of the burial of his body in the cave of Machpelah in Canaan.

It was Jacob's soul, then, that "was gathered unto his people" at the moment of his death and not his body. His soul went to meet the soul of his father Isaac and the soul of his grandfather Abraham. Can there by any doubt, then,

53

about the actual moment that the soul is separated from the body? Is it not at the moment of death? And can there be any doubt that *sheol* is not identical with the grave? One would be blind indeed not to be able to distinguish between *sheol* or hell, the place of the souls or spirits of the departed dead, and *qeber* or *mneemeion*, the place of a dead body.

Sheol is also used in connection with the feeling of desire and various other feelings. In Habakkuk 2:5 we read, "who enlargeth his desire as hell, and is as death, and cannot be satisfied." This is never said to occur in *qeber*. The Jehovah's Witnesses, however, recall here Ecclesiastes 9:10, "Whatsoever thy hand findeth to do, do it with thy might; for there is no work, nor device, nor knowledge, nor wisdom, in the grave *[sheol]*, whither thou goest."

To determine the meaning of this verse, it must be studied in its general context. As we study the whole chapter carefully, we observe that Solomon's general intention is to persuade his readers to do whatever they are able to do while they have the opportunity here on earth, without postponing it for the after-life. Death completely separates the kingdoms of the living and the dead. Whatever you can do in this life you cannot do after death. That is what Solomon says at the end of verse 6: "neither have they any more portion for ever in any thing that is done under the sun."

Another thing; in this passage the writer of Ecclesiastes is concerned with what happens under the sun and what men think, that is, how the dead person appears from the human point of view, and not as he really is. God does not necessarily agree with the acts and conclusions of men, as the Jehovah's Witnesses would have us suppose in this case. The book of Ecclesiastes does not always embody prophecy of the type, "thus saith the Lord," but of the type, "thus thinks man under the sun." The earthly type of living comes to an end with death, and the spirit of man that departs to hell no longer faces the same conditions of life that man did on earth. The conditions are different, but the soul remains alert and "active" and self-conscious.

Where Is Sheol?

We continue our examination of the Old Testament evidence. Twenty out of the sixty-five occurrences of the term *sheol* imply that it is located somewhere "below." In Genesis 37:35 Jacob says, "For I will go down into the grave [*sheol*, hell, incorrectly translated here] unto my son mourning." The same implication may be noted in the New Testament references to hell. In Matthew 11:23 we read, "And thou, Capernaum, which art exalted unto heaven, shalt be brought down to hell." (Cf. Luke 10:15.)

Beyond this indirect implication that *sheol* or hell is located somewhere below, there is no other information in Scripture. Therefore we cannot be dogmatic about something that is not revealed in detail. One thing we know for certain—that *sheol* or hell is a state that man enters after death. Since the soul or spirit of man enters this state without the body, we can assume that this is an immaterial state. As heaven is the "abode" of God, who is Spirit, so *sheol* is the abode of the souls or spirits of the dead. Limited as we are by our humanity, we are unable to think abstractly outside the space-time structures of our present form of existence. That is why we speak of *sheol* or hell as a place. But this is not meant to be taken literally. In calling it a place, we must be careful not to impose on it a meaning it does not have, or rob from it its basic and revealed characteristic of being a spiritual state of existence. The same warning applies to the use of anthropomorphic language in speaking of God.

When the rich man was in hell, he asked that Lazarus be allowed to return to earth to warn his brothers not to come to "this place of torment" (Luke 16:28). As men, we attribute to the term "place" a material existence, but it is possible that "an immaterial place" exists, just as "there is a spiritual body," as Paul says in I Corinthians 15:44. The material designations for immaterial realities is an accommodation to the limitations of our human understanding. Hell, then, is "a spiritual place" that constitutes the abode of the spirits of the dead.

Our observations concerning the Old Testament term of *sheol* apply equally to the New Testament term of hell or *hadees,* which is synonymous with *sheol,* just as the New Testament *mneemeion* is synonymous with the Old Testament *qeber.*

Of the sixty-five occurrences of the word *sheol* in the Old Testament, sixty-one are rendered by the term *hadees* (hell) in the Greek LXX version of the Old Testament. The remaining four are rendered by the word "death," *thanatos* in two instances, and twice by other erroneous terms. The term *sheol* is not once rendered by the term for grave, *mneemeion*. The Modern Greek version published by the British and Foreign Bible Society (known as the Archimandrite Neophytos Bambas Version) erroneously renders *sheol* by the term "grave," *taphos* of Genesis 37:35. Bambas was drawn by the visible side of death and did not observe the invisible side of it. The New Testament refers to many prophecies of the Old Testament, and is, in fact, its best interpreter.

One of these is the Messianic prophecy of Psalm 16:10, "For thou wilt not leave my soul in hell [*sheol*]." Acts 2:27 is a repetition of this prophecy along with its fulfillment in the person of Christ, who had risen from the dead. The word used in the text in Acts is *hadees;* "Thou wilt not leave my soul in *hadees.*"

The word *mneemeion* (grave, tomb) occurs in its plural form in ten instances. The word *hadees* is never used in the plural: We read, for example, about the "new tomb' of Joseph of Arimathaea (Matt. 27:60). We also read that the dead body of John the Baptist was taken by his disciples and "laid . . . in a tomb" (Mark 6:29). This was apparently a special tomb. In the time of Jesus, tombs were built and decorated for the bodies of the dead. Among the sayings of Jesus recorded in the Gospels there is one that refers to the Pharisaic habit of building tombs for the prophets. "Woe unto you, scribes and Pharisees, hypocrites! because ye build the tombs of the prophets, and garnish the sepulchres of the righteous" (Matt. 23:29). This kind of language is never used for *hadees*. *Hadees* does not belong to one man or another, nor can it be seen in one place or another.

The *mneemeion* (tomb) has a definite geographical position. "And the graves were opened; and many bodies of the saints which slept arose, and came out of the graves after his resurrection, and went into the holy city, and appeared unto many" (Matt. 27:52, 53). This shows that the graves were located in the circumference of Jerusalem. "Now in the place where he [Jesus] was crucified there was a garden; and in the garden a new sepulchre, wherein was never man yet laid" (John 19:41). This kind of precise geographical placement is never attributed to hell. The tomb is the place where the body of a dead person is placed. "And the women also, which came with him from Galilee, followed after, and beheld the sepulchre, and how his body was laid" (Luke 23:55). But *hadees* is never said to be the recipient of the body, because it is related only to the spirit or soul of man.

A seeming exception occurs in the 16th chapter of Luke, where Christ speaks about the state of the rich man and Lazarus in the after-life. "And in hell he [the rich man] lift up his eyes" (v. 23). We are not to suppose that the rich man possessed physical eyes, of the same type that he possessed on earth. This is rather a metaphorical expression, indicating that in the after-life in hell man is fully aware of his environment. He is conscious that he suffers and is aware of what takes place around him. His existence is personal but not necessarily physical. Scriptures are full of such metaphorical representations. Christ Himself said that God is a Spirit (John 4:24), and yet Scripture speaks about His back, His face, His eyes, His nostrils, His feet, His hands, and so on. These are symbolic of the various activities or operations of God's personality and should not be taken literally, as though God's being was anthropomorphic. "The eyes of the Lord are upon the righteous, and his ears are open unto their cry. The face of the Lord is against them that do evil, to cut off the remembrance of them from the earth" (Ps. 34:15, 16).

There is more Scriptural evidence that shows that *mneemeion* (grave or tomb) and *hadees* (hell) are two entirely different things. We think, however, that the evidence so far presented is sufficient. We have demonstrated from Scripture that the tomb or grave is the earthly place of repose for the dead body of man, while hell (*hadees*) is a state or a "place" that receives the immaterial part of man, his soul or spirit, when he dies. Those who continue to assert that *sheol* or *hadees* are synonymous with *qeber* or *mneemeion* become irrational and in the final analysis pervert and twist the truth of God's Word. It is to be regretted that many people are misled by their specious arguments. But the prevalence of these irrational and perverse teachers should not take us by surprise. The Apostle Paul has warned us prophetically against them. "But evil men and seducers shall wax worse and worse, deceiving, and being deceived" (II Tim. 3:13).

Incorruption, Incorruptibility, Immortality

To avoid confusion and misunderstanding of the Scriptural statements referring to death, it is necessary to clarify the precise meaning of the various relevant terms.

I Corinthians 15:53: "For this corruptible must put on incorruption, and this mortal must put on immortality."

I Corinthians 15:54: "So when this corruptible shall have put on incorruption, and this mortal shall have put on immortality, then shall be brought to pass the saying that is written, Death is swallowed up in victory."

I Timothy 6:16: "Who [Christ] only hath immortality, dwelling in the light which no man can approach unto; whom no man hath seen, nor can see: to whom be honour and power everlasting. Amen."

The word "incorruption" is used in relation to the body of the resurrection in the two quotations from I Corinthians, as well as in verses 42 and 50 of that same chapter: "So also is the resurrection of the dead. It is sown in corruption; it is raised in incorruption . . . . Now this I say, brethren, that flesh and blood cannot inherit the kingdom of God; neither doth corruption inherit incorruption."

Romans 2:7: "To them who by patient continuance in well doing seek for . . . immortality." The Greek word translated "immortality" here is *aphtharsia,* which should more accurately be rendered "incorruption."

II Timothy 1:10: "Jesus Christ, who hath abolished death, and hath brought life and immortality to light through the gospel." The work translated "immortality" here is *aphtharsian,* which again should have been translated "incorruption."

Nowhere does the Bible state that the soul is immortal or possesses immortality. Of course, we are not to conclude from this that the soul dies, for the soul never ceases to exist. Whenever we commonly use the term, "the immortality of the soul," we actually mean just what the Bible teaches, that it is eternal. But this eternal quality of the soul is never designated as immortality in the Scriptures. Man, as soul or spirit, continues to exist after the death of the body. Again, Scripture never calls this immortality. Our common terminology is quite different from the Scriptural terminology.

The Bible does not teach that the soul of man actually dies, if by the term "dies" we refer

63

to cessation of existence. When it speaks of spiritual death, it means the separation of man's soul from God. Since the spirit or soul of man constitutes the immaterial part of human existence, it is to be understood that spiritual death— separation from God, not cessation of existence—refers to the soul or spirit. The term "death" in Scripture never means extinction but simply separation. Spiritual death is separation of the soul from God, and physical death is separation of the soul from the body. (See also chapter 5 of this book.)

The soul is not immortal, morally speaking. It does die spiritually, in that it is separated from God because of sin. But this does not mean that it ceases to exist, but that it is estranged from its Creator. This is the direct consequence of sin. Man continues, however, to have an everlasting conscious existence. It is with this meaning that the word "death" is used in relation to the soul or spirit in the following verses:

Ezekiel 18:4: "The soul that sinneth, it shall die."

Romans 6:23: "For the wages of sin is death; but the gift of God is eternal life through Jesus Christ our Lord."

Ephesians 2:1: "And you hath he quickened, who were dead in trespasses and sins."

Christ is the only One of whom Scripture says that He possesses immortality. And He possesses this only in His divinity. Jesus Christ as God the Son was never separated from God the Father. In His incarnation, however, He was forsaken on the cross for our sakes. What sin was able to do to us, it did to Him also. This is why He cried out, "My God, my God, why hast thou forsaken me?" (Matthew 27:46). Thus Jesus died a physical death, and also as man He suffered the consequences of sin—the instant separation of His Spirit from His Father's Spirit, without however experiencing sin itself, either hereditary from Adam or personal, as we do.

Physical death does not put an end to man's existence; it simply brings about a change from a bodily existence to a bodiless existence. Immortality is not a gift of God that is equal to eternal life. After death, both the righteous and the unrighteous continue to have conscious existence. But eternal life is a gift that only those who believe in Christ possess. The life of God in the soul of man is a spiritual state that reconciles man to God.

The two terms, "immortality" *(athanasia)* and "incorruption" *(aphtharsia),* as referred to in Scripture, have nothing to do with the spiritual makeup of man but only with his physical makeup, his body. The body is mortal and therefore deteriorates or becomes corrupt. The continuing deterioration of the body during life finally brings about its death, which is its separation from the soul.

One day our bodies will be clothed with immortality and incorruption—qualities they do not possess in this life. This will take place at the resurrection. The Apostle Paul makes this clear when he says in I Corinthians 15:52, "The trumpet shall sound, and the dead shall be raised incorruptible [the resurrection bodies], and we shall be changed." This means that those who are dead will receive new incorruptible bodies, and those who are alive will have their present bodies changed to acquire incorruptibility. It is in that new state that our bodies will experience no sickness and pain in contrast to what they go through now.

The new bodies that our souls will acquire will be different from our present ones. They will be incorruptible, which means they will not deteriorate. "For this corruptible must put on incorruption, and this mortal must put on immortality . . . . then shall be brought to pass the saying that is written, Death is swallowed up in victory" (I Corinthians 15:53, 54). Never again will our resurrection bodies be separated from our souls, as happened at death. This is the immortality that our new state will enjoy.

However, the second part of I Corinthians 15:51 speaks of those who are still alive at the coming of the Lord. Paul says, "We shall not all sleep, but we shall all be changed." Those who are alive when the Lord comes will automatically receive immortality and incorruption. They do not need to be resurrected, but simply to have their bodies transformed. These will cease being corruptible and mortal, and will become incorruptible and immortal.

Thus all believers, dead and alive at the coming of the Lord, will have bodies similar to the glorious body of the risen Christ, "who shall change our vile body [the Greek here is 'the body of our humiliation'], that it may be fashioned like unto his glorious body, according to the working whereby he is able even to subdue all things unto himself" (Philippians 3:21).

We therefore conclude that no believer now has an immortal body. The only one who possesses incorruptibility and immortality is the Lord Jesus Christ, whose body never saw corruption, as promised in Psalm 16:10: "For thou wilt not leave my soul in hell; neither wilt thou suffer thine Holy One to see corruption." That the term "corruption" refers to Christ's body is made clear by what the Apostle Peter said in his sermon at Pentecost: "He seeing this before spake of the resurrection of Christ, that his soul was not left in hell *[hadees]*, neither his flesh did see corruption *[diaphthorans]*" (Acts 2:31).

The Scriptural statement that Christ is the only One who has immortality, as Paul states in I Timothy 6:16, means that Christ in His eternal state as God also possessed the quality of immortality apart from His incarnation. But even His mortal body has already clothed itself with immortality. We can therefore truly say that He became the firstfruits of the resurrection of the dead. What happened to Him will also take place in us who are His. In II Timothy 1:10 the Apostle Paul tells us that when Christ appears He will abolish death. This means that the dead will be clothed with immortality and the living will be transformed so that they will be similarly clothed. His appearance will bring life and incorruption to light through the Gospel.

Incorruptibility and immortality in the New Testament do not pertain to our present state but to the future. In Romans 2:6, 7 Paul says that God "will render to every man according to his deeds: to them who by patient continuance in well doing seek for glory and honour and immortality [*aphtharsian,* incorruptibility], eternal life." The Apostle Peter says the same thing when he refers to "an inheritance incorruptible, and undefiled, and that fadeth not away, reserved in heaven for you" (I Peter 1:4).

We see that only when immortality and incorruptibility refer to God are they mentioned as present possessions, and not as something relegated to the future. "Who only hath [present tense] immortality" (I Timothy 6:16). And I Timothy 1:17 says, "Now unto the King eternal, immortal [*aphthartoo,* incorruptible], invisible, the only wise God, be [now, at this present time] honour and glory for ever and ever."

The contrast between God and men in this

respect is indicated in Romans 1:23, which speaks of the heathen who "changed the glory of the uncorruptible God into an image made like to corruptible man, and to birds, and fourfooted beasts, and creeping things." (See also the chapter in this book entitled "The Resurrection Body.")

What Is Hadees?

During Old Testament times, as well as when the Lord Jesus Christ was down here on earth, *sheol* or *hadees* was the common dwelling place of the spirits of the righteous and the unrighteous dead.

As we study Luke 16:19-31, we conclude that both the rich man and Lazarus, the one unrighteous and the other righteous, went to *hadees* when they died. In verse 23 we see that the rich man was suffering in *hadees:* "And in *hadees* he lift up his eyes, being in torments." Observe that we translated the word *hadees* exactly as it is found in the Greek text. It is not "hell" as the Authorized Version has it. *Hadees,* therefore, is shown to be a state of torment. It is an actual place (verse 28): "lest they also come into this place of torment." We conclude, therefore, that *hadees* is both a state and a place.

From that section of *hadees* where the unrighteous man was, he could see righteous Lazarus, whom he had ignored in life. He also saw the patriarch of the faith, Abraham, and even spoke with him. But it is evident that the section of *hadees* where the rich man was, was separate from the section where these righteous persons were. Abraham and Lazarus were not suffering but were being comforted. This place of comfort was called "Abraham's bosom" (verse 22).

These two places within *hadees* were separated by a great gulf: "Between us and you there is a great gulf fixed," said Abraham, "so that they which would pass from hence to you cannot; neither can they pass to us, that would come from thence" (verse 26). Don't believe anyone who claims to have the power to transfer you from one place to the other, especially if his prayers are being paid for. Once you die, your fate is sealed. There can be no hope of improving your eternal state after death. It is only in this life that you have a chance to repent. Your eternal destiny is determined by your decision while on earth. Faith in Christ which is followed by the works of faith means a life of eternal comfort. Unbelief, with its consequent indifference to God and the plight of others, means eternal torment. The decision is yours here and now.

But the Bible also teaches that the soul or spirit of Christ went to *hadees* when He died. This information was given to us first as a prophecy in Psalm 16:10, "For thou wilt not leave my soul in *sheol;* neither wilt thou suffer thine Holy One to see corruption." Peter, in his sermon on the day of Pentecost, referred to this prophecy and its fulfillment in the person of the risen Christ: "Because thou wilt not leave my soul in *hadees,* neither wilt thou suffer thine Holy One to see corruption" (Acts 2:27). "He seeing this before spake of the resurrection of Christ, that his soul was not left in *hadees,* neither his flesh did see corruption" (Acts 2:31). Christ went to *hadees* but He did not remain there. These verses, however, do not state in which of the two sections of *hadees* Christ went.

Let us listen to Christ on the cross. When the repentant thief proclaimed faith in Him, Jesus said, "Verily I say unto thee, To day shalt thou be with me in paradise" (Luke 23:43). Paradise was undoubtedly the place of the righteous ones in *hadees.* That's where the Lord Himself also went. Therefore "Abraham's bosom" and paradise are synonymous terms referring to the place of rest and comfort for the righteous dead.

Before the resurrection of Christ, it would seem that *hadees* was the place where all the dead—righteous and unrighteous—went. However, after Christ's resurrection, which inaugurated the new fuller proclamation of God's grace, we never find any reference in the New Testament to any righteous person descending into *hadees.* The spirits of the righteous dead are always mentioned as ascending to be with Christ in the heavens.

Every Sunday, millions of English-speaking

Christians repeat the Apostles' Creed. Among other things they affirm belief in Jesus Christ, who "suffered" and was "buried" and "descended into hell." This last phrase is unfortunate. The Scriptural phraseology in the Greek New Testament is, "And he descended into the lower parts of the earth" (Ephesians 4:9). The phrase about Christ descending into hell does not occur in any of the ancient manuscripts of the Apostles' Creed. It represents an addition that seems to have come into the picture at the beginning of the sixth century. This was an addition to the creed that was used by the Western Church. It seems to have been made by one Rufinus of Aquileia, who incorporated this into the Creed as part of a confession of faith. He himself, however, does not mention the fact that this addition to the Creed was made to the Creed of Rome until the end of the fourth century.

It is interesting to note that in the creeds of Nicaea and Constantinople this addition does not occur. It is strange indeed that the first appearance of the phrase about Christ descending into hell was at a synod of the Arians (the heretics who denied the deity of Christ), at Sirmion of Pannonia, at Nicaea and Constantinople, and during the years 359 to 360. The general impression derived from these statements is that the Lord on dying descended to the dwelling place of departed spirits to visit them and to teach the patriarchs and prophets of the Old Testament.

This view is often apparent in the writings of the Church Fathers. According to Tertullian, "No one enters heaven before the end of the world." To him paradise was part of a place in the lower parts of the earth, as it appears in the account of Luke 16:19-31, but it does not constitute the final dwelling place of the faithful.

Here is what most of the Church Fathers from A.D. 150 to 400 believed about Christ and His relationship to *hadees*. After His death, Christ descended into the depths of the earth—the dwelling place of the spirits of the death—and there He preached to the saints and the patriarchs of the Old Testament. At this time He liberated them from captivity in the lower parts of *hadees* from which Christians, and especially those who suffered martyrdom, later were exempt. Christ translated these saints to paradise, the higher part of *hadees,* to which faithful Christians go immediately at death.

It is quite possible that the Church Fathers were greatly influenced by I Peter 4:6, "For this cause was the gospel preached also to them that are dead, that they might be judged according to men in the flesh, but live according to God in the spirit," and also by I Peter 3:18, 19: "For Christ also hath once suffered for sins, the just for the unjust, that he might bring us to God, being put to death in the flesh, but quickened by the Spirit: by which also he went and preached unto the spirits in prison."

In II Corinthians 12:2, Paul refers to the occasion when he himself was caught up to the third heaven. And in verse 4 he says, "He was caught up into paradise, and heard unspeakable words." According to the revelation we have here, therefore, the third heaven and paradise are synonymous. They are located "up" and not "down" as is *hadees.*

We have no reason to contradict this view. The general teaching of the Scriptures is that at death the spirit returns to God who gave it and who dwells in the heavens (Ecclesiastes 12:7). This is confirmed by the fact that when that first martyr of the Christian faith, Stephen, died, he called upon Christ, who was and is in the heavens, to receive his spirit (Acts 7:56, 59).

Paul also expresses a desire to depart from this world and to be with Christ, where it is much better (Philippians 1:23). Therefore the place of comfort and joy—paradise—according to Scripture is somewhere above, while *hadees* is somewhere below. It is impossible, however, to determine exactly where this "up" and "down" are.

There are some who have projected the following theory: When Christ descended into *hadees* after His death on the cross, He joined the righteous ones of the Old Testament who were in some way captives there. When He rose from the dead, He liberated them and transferred them from *hadees* to heaven, where since that time all the faithful ones go. This theory is based upon

Ephesians 4:8-10, which states: "When he ascended up on high, he led captivity captive, and gave gifts unto men. (Now that he ascended, what is it but that he also descended first into the lower parts of the earth? He that descended is the same also that ascended up far above all heavens, that he might fill all things.)"

We seriously doubt the correctness of this theory, because it is not cleary set forth in the Bible. There may be value to it, but we do not see it clearly supported by Scripture. We cannot interpret passages that may refer to such a theory independently of their context. We must recognize what is the main topic of discussion in Ephesians 4:7-16, before assigning a meaning to verses 8-10.

The Apostle Paul speaks in these verses about the gifts Christ gave to His Church and to those who minister in the building up of His body. In John 16:7, 13, 14 and Acts 2:33, we find that Christ gave gifts to men through the Holy Spirit. It is these gifts that the Lord took unto Himself as if they were His captives. They became His possession, by virtue of His victory on the cross, the triumph of His resurrection, and His ascension into heaven. This capturing of the gifts did not become a reality in *hadees,* to which He descended, but in the heights of Heaven where He entered as a Victor. This is why Paul says, "He that descended is the same also that ascended up far above all heavens." It is there that He led captivity captive, that is to say, he gave gifts unto men.

The gifts of the Holy Spirit were captured by Christ as the conqueror and became His possession. This is what Ephesians 4:7-16 is all about. And this is why Peter said on the day of Pentecost, "Therefore being by the right hand of God exalted, and having received of the Father the promise of the Holy Ghost, he hath shed forth this, which ye now see and hear" (Acts 2:33). In other words, the demonstration of the Holy Spirit and His gifts on the day of Pentecost was due to the exaltation of Christ in heaven.

For these reasons we cannot find any justification for the popular interpretation of Ephesians 4:8-10 that Christ descended to *hadees* and transferred the spirits of the faithful dead to paradise or heaven. Of course, we don't exclude the possibility of something like that, but it has not been clearly revealed in Scripture. At least Ephesians 4:8-10 doesn't declare this truth clearly, and therefore we must express our personal doubts about the correctness of this interpretation.

It is clear, however, from the definite examples we are given in the New Testament of Stephen and Paul that, during the new order of the proclamation of God's grace initiated by the resurrection and the ascension of Christ to heaven, the believers in Christ, when they die, no longer go to *hadees* but are with Christ in the heavens (see Hebrews 12:23). The whole New Testament supports with certainty the fact that when the righteous die they go to be where Christ is. And we know that Christ is not now in *hadees* but in heaven, to which He ascended.

Does Man Become
"Extinct" at Death? (Part 1)

We have already shown that at death the spirit or soul of man is separated from his body, and that, ever since the time of Christ's ascension, the spirits of the righteous dead enter into the presence of Christ in paradise or the third heaven. The spirits of the unrighteous dead go to *hadees,* which now belongs exclusively to them.

The next question that arises is whether the departed spirits are in a state of consciousness. Do the spirits or soul of the dead sleep as their bodies sleep, or do they know what is going on? Are they conscious of their environment?

The greater part of Christendom believes that after death the soul or spirit of man continues to live on, fully conscious of itself and its environment. But there are some who believe that the soul becomes unconscious, is extinguished, sleeps. And these people tell us that such a state will continue till the resurrection.

In reality this doctrine is the natural consequence of their belief that the soul or spirit is not a separate entity as distinguished from the body, but is merely man's physical breath. Since they do not believe that the soul exists during man's physical life as a separate entity, they do not believe it exists after his physical death.

They base this theory on a few Old Testament Scriptures. One of these is Psalm 115:17, "The dead praise not the Lord, neither any that go down into silence."

According to them, the Bible teaches that when man dies he doesn't know anything; he is simply extinct. We answer that the Bible teaches no such thing. When man dies, whether he is righteous or unrighteous, he continues to exist, but under a different form from that which he possessed in life, and in an entirely different environment.

A grave error of these people who misinterpret the Scriptures is the isolation of certain verses from their context. In studying any portion of Scripture we should always ask three basic questions: 1) Who makes this declaration: a man who is setting down his own thoughts, or God speaking through His prophets and apostles? (In the case of Job's "comforters," although their statements are set down in the Bible, God declares that they were in error.) 2), To whom are such declarations addressed? And 3) do such declarations concern something that is of local character or are they of universal application?

Let's examine Psalm 115:17 cited by the Jehovah's Witnesses in support of their theory: "The dead praise not the Lord, neither any that go down into silence." First consider the context. In the verse that immediately follows, we understand that the Psalmist is telling us that, if we do not praise God while we are down here on earth, we shall not be able to do it in our existence after death. He says in verse 18, "But we will bless the Lord from this time forth and for evermore." If we praise God now, in this life, we shall continue to praise Him even after death. Our attitude toward God in the afterlife will be the projection of our present attitude in this life. What we do now we shall do hereafter, and what we are now (that is, righteous or unrighteous) we shall be hereafter. It is impossible for us to curse God here and praise Him in the hereafter.

When the Psalmist says, "The dead praise not the Lord, neither any that go down into silence," He speaks about the unbelieving dead. Then he goes on to speak about the believers, saying what they do now and what they will do in eternity. "But we will bless the Lord from this time forth and for evermore." We bless the Lord now and we shall ever bless Him throughout eternity. Thus we dispose of the first error of the Jehovah's Witnesses.

Now we come to another passage they misinterpret, Ecclesiastes 9:5, 10: "For the living know that they shall die: but the dead know not any thing, neither have they any more a reward; for the memory of them is forgotten . . . . Whatsoever thy hand findeth to do, do it with thy might; for there is no work, nor device, nor knowledge, nor wisdom, in *sheol,* whither thou goest."

Let's take a look at the context of these verses, beginning with verses 4-6. The writer of Ecclesiastes, King Solomon, speaks of the impossibility of any relationship between the living and the dead, and vice versa. The living cannot do what the dead do, nor can the dead do whatever the living do.

"For to him that is joined to all the living there is hope [that is, for the living person there is still hope; no such hope exists for the dead]: for a living dog is better than a dead lion. For the living know that they shall die: but the dead know not any thing, neither have they any more a reward; for the memory of them is forgotten. Also their love, and their hatred, and their envy, is now perished; neither have they any more a portion for ever in any thing that is done under the sun."

These verses tell us that death does not put an end to the existence of man, but only to his earthly activity. His love and his hatred do not influence the living as they did when he was alive. He does not forever have a share of all that takes place under the sun.

Furthermore, let's not forget that Solomon

does not claim that he is transmitting divine revelation here. By the Holy Spirit's inspiration, he simply gives accurate expression to the common thoughts of man, and what is taking place in the life of man from the human viewpoint, without necessarily approving them. He tells us how the common man thinks "under the sun," that is, in this life. In his short book, he repeats this expression 29 times. In Ecclesiastes 9:9, 10, he gives us a summary of exactly how the man of the world thinks:

"Live joyfully with the wife whom thou lovest all the days of the life of thy vanity, which he hath given thee under the sun, all the days of thy vanity: for that is thy portion in this life, and in thy labour which thou takest under the sun." The worldly man thinks only of the enjoyment of earthly good. Why? Because he doesn't believe in the life to come. Anyone who doesn't believe in a future judgment will live only for the things of this world. Therefore the man "under the sun" says to himself, "Whatsoever thy hand findeth to do, do it with thy might; for there is no work, nor device, nor knowledge, nor wisdom in *sheol*, whither thou goest."

It's clear that it isn't God who says such a thing, but the common sinful man. The philosophy of the earthly minded to this day is "Let us eat and drink; for to morrow we die" (I Cor. 15:32). And of course they believe that death brings an end to everything.

In the last chapter of Ecclesiastes, Solomon leaves behind the thoughts of man "under the sun" and ascends to the higher stages of divine revelation when he says categorically, "Then shall the dust return to the earth as it was: and the spirit shall return unto God who gave it" (12:7).

Does Man Become
"Extinct" at Death? (Part 2)

The New Testament makes it very clear that the physical death of man doesn't mean his extinction. The Apostle Paul tells us that Christ is the One who abolished death and brought to light life and immortality through the Gospel (II Timothy 1:10). The coming of Christ shed some light on this dark subject of our future state. Let's see what that light reveals.

First, the New Testament proclaims that those who now enjoy physical life but are unregenerated are "dead," spiritually dead, that is. "And you hath he quickened [made alive], who were dead in trespasses and sins" (Ephesians 2:1). Scripture declares unbelievers are "dead," but that doesn't mean they've ceased to exist. Do you recall what that joyful father said when his prodigal son returned from a far country? "For this my son was dead, and is alive again; he was lost, and is found" (Luke 15:24). He was dead, yet he existed.

Again this confirms the fact that the basic

meaning of death is separation. Just as this prodigal was considered "dead" when separated by sin and distance from his father, so the person who is said to be spiritually dead is one who is separated from God. His spirit and God's Spirit are not related. A person who is physically dead is one whose spirit or soul is separated from his body; but that spirit or soul continues to exist in its disembodied state.

There are those who believe that the soul of man sleeps after death. They base this theory on the fact that in the New Testament the dead are said to "sleep." Though death is called sleep, this doesn't mean non-existence but a state of expectancy in which their souls or spirits look forward to the resurrection. When you sleep you don't cease to exist; you simply don't have full consciousness of your environment. This refers only to the body, for in sleep you think, you dream, you exist. This is why a man on awaking from sleep refers to his dreaming state as a condition of estrangement from his environment. Nevertheless, in sleep the soul exists and thinks. In fact, sleep frequently brings to the surface much that has been hidden in the area of the subconscious. Sleep has a way of reviving memory.

Let's examine New Testament passages that use the term "sleep" to indicate the death of the body, to see if this includes extinction of personality or is simply the separation of man's spiritual being from his material being.

86

Take John 11:11-14, which deals with Lazarus. When messengers came to tell Christ of his illness, He knew Lazarus was already dead. But He said to His disciples, "Our friend Lazarus sleepeth; but I go, that I may awake him out of sleep." The disciples didn't understand this as a symbolic reference to death. They thought Lazarus had fallen into a restful slumber. This is why the Lord said plainly, "Lazarus is dead."

When Christ subsequently raised Lazarus, was it his soul or his body that He raised? It was his body of course. And in order to accomplish this it was necessary for his soul to be reunited with his body, from which it had been separated at death. His body had already been in the tomb four days. The fact that the two terms "sleepeth" and "died" refer to Lazarus' body is apparent from what his sister Martha said: "He stinketh" (John 11:39). It is obvious, therefore, that the sleep or death of Lazarus referred only to his body and not to his soul or spirit.

Now let's consider Matthew 27:52. This refers to the hour when the body of Christ expired on the cross. "And the graves were opened; and many bodies of the saints which slept arose." Those that slept were the dead. What was in the grave? Their bodies. It is the bodies that were raised. It follows, therefore, that it is not the soul which sleeps, but the body, when man dies.

Acts 7:54-60 refers to the stoning to death

of Stephen. "And when he had said this, he fell asleep," that is to say, he died. What slept? What died? His body or his soul? His body, of course. What happened to his spirit? He delivered it to the Lord whom he saw "standing on the right hand of God." He said, "Lord Jesus, receive my spirit." Why deliver his spirit to Christ if that spirit became extinct at death?

I Corinthians 15:20: This whole 15th chapter deals with the resurrection of the body of Christ and consequently of the believers. "But now is Christ risen from the dead, and become the firstfruits of them that slept." Those that slept are the dead, but it isn't their souls that died, but their bodies. (The reader is referred to the author's 860-page expository study of the 15th chapter of I Corinthians entitled *Conquering the Fear of Death*.)

Scripture never teaches that the soul or spirit separated from the body sleeps, and this is merely a figure of speech indicating the outward similarity of a corpse to a sleeping person. Even in those who are physically alive, Scripture teaches that separation of their souls or spirits from God is spiritual death. Adam died spiritually the moment he sinned, that is, when he disobeyed God. What the devil promised Eve, in Genesis 3:4, that they would not die, was not true. Man died spiritually. From that moment on his soul was estranged from his Creator, God. As man, however, he continued to exist, to live in the physical realm. As a result of his sin, however, Ezekiel's later prophecy proved to be true, "The soul that sinneth, it shall die" (Ezekiel 18:4, 20).

The Jehovah's Witnesses use this verse as if it meant that the soul that sins ceases to exist. But that would be no punishment. God's attitude toward sin is one of punishment, especially when man rejects Christ's offer of redemption. If we examine the verses that follow, we shall see that they speak of the righteous man and the blessing God brings upon him (see Ezekiel 18:5, 20b).

The soul that sins is separated from God and dies in its relationship to God and His blessing. Again this doesn't mean it ceases to exist. Many times the Bible uses the term "soul" to indicate man as a unit, as his present personality made up of both body and soul. (See Acts 27:22, 37; 7:14, I Peter 3:20.)

God had said to Adam, "In the day that thou eatest thereof thou shalt surely die" (Genesis 2:17). Yet Adam did not die physically on the day of his fall. He was put out of paradise, however, and separated from God. That was what God meant by His warning—Adam's moral death, the death of his soul, which no longer had communion with God, even though it continued to exist along with his body.

The State of the Soul
after Death (Part 1)

We have already shown from Scripture that death separates the spirit or soul of man from his body. We have also seen that the soul or spirit of a righteous person, one born again by the Spirit of God, goes to the third heaven, to paradise, while the soul or spirit of an unsaved person goes to *hadees.* Now we must find out what is the state of the souls or spirits of dead believers and unbelievers. Are they conscious or unconscious?

In the story of Lazarus and the rich man in Luke 16:19-31, we see that the souls of both these men after death were conscious of what was going on with them and around them. Jesus Christ Himself has assured us that the state of the soul after death is one of consciousness.

Some people, in order to justify their unscriptural theories, maintain that this is only a parable and not a real incident or event. However, the context does not state that this is a parable. When Christ taught in parables, He either said so, or the context indicated this. For instance, Matthew 13:3 says, "And he spake many things unto them in parables saying . . . ." (See also Matt. 20:1; 22:1, Luke 13:18; 15:3, etc.) But even if this is a parable, its lessons must be true concerning the condition of the soul after death, because the Lord, even when speaking in parables, was illustrating real truths and events. It is noteworthy that in none of His parables did the Lord mention any real names. Yet in this account in Luke 16 He names Lazarus, and further particularizes the rich man as having five brothers on earth.

Now let's go on to examine other verses:

Matthew 10:28: "And fear not them which kill the body, but are not able to kill the soul: but rather fear him which is able to destroy both soul and body in hell." Christ very clearly says here that when the body is killed the soul doesn't die at the same time.

Matthew 17:3: This concerns the transfiguration of Christ, on the occasion when two people who had left this earthly life a long time ago, Moses and Elijah, appeared before Him and His three disciples. "And, behold, there appeared unto them Moses and Elias talking with him." How could this happen if their spirits did not exist? We therefore conclude that man's spirit thinks, speaks, and recognizes after death.

Hebrews 12:1: This chapter of the Epistle to the Hebrews cites the faith and example of the saints who lived in the past. "Wherefore seeing we also are compassed about with so great a cloud of witnesses . . . ." Were these witnesses living or dead? We know that their bodies were dead, but their souls were alive. Otherwise what good was their testimony? These martyrs were enjoying the reward of their faith. The example of their faith is mentioned so that we might be established and strengthened, as verse 3 tells us: "Lest ye be wearied and faint in your minds [*souls* in the Greek text]."

Where are these witnesses now? The writer of Hebrews tells us in verse 23 that they are "the general assembly and church of the firstborn, which are written in heaven . . . the spirits of just men made perfect."

In the New Testament the term "eternal life" is used repeatedly. Eternal life is the life of God, which therefore can never be said to end. Physical death cannot possibly eliminate this eternal life. In this connection, let's consider the following verses:

John 3:36: "He that believeth on the Son hath everlasting life."

John 5:24: "Verily, verily, I say unto you, He that heareth my word, and believeth on him that sent me, hath everlasting life."

This eternal life is our present possession if we are believers. We can never lose it; not even death can deprive us of it. Many of the results of our earthly efforts, which occupy us so wholeheartedly, will perish. Not the eternal life, however, which is offered to us freely by Christ if we believe in Him.

John 10:28-30: "And I give unto them eternal life; and they shall never perish, neither shall any man pluck them out of my hand." Not even death can do this.

John 11:25, 26: In speaking to Martha, Christ said, "I am the resurrection, and the life: he that believeth in me, though he were dead, yet shall he live." Lazarus had already died. But he lived spiritually. His soul and spirit had not been extinguished. "And whosoever liveth and believeth in me shall never die." Christ had assured Martha that Lazarus had died as far as his body was concerned, but not his soul.

Luke 20:27, 37, 38: These verses speak to us about a discussion Christ had with the Sadducees. These people did not believe in the resurrection or in life after death, and they wanted to question Christ about this. The Sadducees were a Hebrew sect that believed in the extinction of body and soul after death. Josephus, a highly educated Hebrew historian of that day, wrote: "The doctrine of the Sadducees is this, that the souls die with the body" (*Antiquities* B28:4). "They reject the faith in the immortal existence of the soul, as well as the punishments and the rewards of *hadees*" (*Wars* B8:14).

What was Christ's reply to the Sadducees? Did He agree that they would cease to exist after death? In Luke 20:35-38 He says: "But they which shall be accounted worthy to obtain that world, and the resurrection from the dead, neither marry, nor are given in marriage: neither can they die any more: for they are equal unto the angels; and are the children of God, being the children of the resurrection. Now that the dead are raised, even Moses shewed at the bush, when he calleth the Lord the God of Abraham, and the God of Isaac, and the God of Jacob. For he is not a God of the dead, but of the living: for all live unto him.''

Note that Luke tells us in Acts 23:8, ''The Sadducees say that there is no resurrection, neither angel, nor spirit.'' The Sadducees believed that when they died they ceased to be. Since they did not believe in the spirit as a separate entity from the body, it was natural for them not to believe that the spirit could live on after the death of the body. This is why our Lord cited the example of Moses at the burning bush. When he faced God, the Lord said to him, ''I am the God of thy father, the God of Abraham, the God of Isaac, and the God of Jacob'' (Exodus 3:6). This was about 1449 years before Christ was born in Bethlehem. Abraham died in the year 1995 B.C., or thereabouts, Isaac in 1885 B.C. or thereabouts, and Jacob in 1858 or so B.C. Therefore, about 1449 B.C., when the Lord spoke to Moses, Abraham had been dead for about 546 years, Isaac for about 436 years, and Jacob for about 409 years. Nevertheless, God told Moses that He was the God of these three persons who, although they had physically died, He considered alive.

Consider what He said—not, "I *was* the God of Abraham, Isaac, and Jacob," but "I *am* the God of Abraham, Isaac, and Jacob." Therefore, when these three patriarchs of the Old Testament died, they did not lapse into extinction but continued to enjoy a spiritual existence separated from their earthly bodies.

Why did our Lord cite an example taken from the Pentateuch to prove His point? He was speaking to the Sadducees, and they accepted only the Pentateuch as the inspired Word of God. Therefore, if Christ could prove to them from the Pentateuch that there was a resurrection of the dead, and that the spirits of men lived on after death, they would be obliged to accept this as incontrovertible proof. Furthermore, Christ considered these two doctrines—the resurrection of the dead and the continued existence of the soul in a conscious state after its separation from the body—as inseparable truths. God could not be a God of people who had ceased to exist.

The Sadducees were left without an answer. "And after that they durst not ask him any question at all" (Luke 20:40). Our prayer is that the present followers of the Sadducees may also see and acknowledge their error and follow the doctrine of Christ, that God is a God of the living, and all who believe in Him live in Him.

The State of the Soul after Death (Part 2)

The Apostle Paul declared that we who are in Christ when we die do not cease to exist but enter into the presence of the Lord Jesus Christ. For instance in II Corinthians 5:6-8 he says, "Therefore we are always confident, knowing that, whilst we are at home in the body, we are absent from the Lord: (For we walk by faith, not sight:) We are confident, I say, and willing rather to be absent from the body, and to be present with the Lord." We depart from the body only when we die. Paul equates this with our entrance into the presence of the Lord. He does not voice this merely as a pious hope; he stresses it as a fact: "We are confident, knowing. . . ." He was absolutely sure of it.

Paul nowhere intimates that his death would bring cessation of his personal being. If he were to be no more when he died, why did he express such a great desire to die? He knew with assurance that he would be in the presence of the Lord, in full consciousness of his blessed state forever. If he were not to have a conscious existence in the presence of the Lord, how could he possibly enjoy His presence?

The same truth is also apparent in Philippians 1:21, 23, 24, where the same apostle says, "For to me to live is Christ, and to die is gain. . . . For I am in a strait betwixt two, having a desire to depart, and to be with Christ; which is far better: nevertheless, to abide in the flesh is more needful for you." If death meant non-existence, how could he possibly count such an experience "gain"?

Luke 23:42, 43: When our Lord was dying on the cross, one of the two thieves said to Him, "Lord, remember me when thou comest into thy kingdom." Did Christ reply that he would have to wait until Christ came back to establish His Kingdom? No. "Jesus said unto him, Verily I say unto thee, To day shalt thou be with me in paradise." This clearly teaches that the thief was not going to cease existing as an individual personality, but that he would continue to exist immediately after his death, that very day.

Those who do not believe in the conscious existence of the spirit of man when he dies say that there should be a comma after the word "today," making "today" relate to "I tell you" instead of to "shalt thou be with me in paradise." This is completely illogical. Why would anyone need to say, "I tell you today"? There is no need to specify when the speaking is done. When one uses the present tense, he does not have to say,

"I am speaking to you now." This is redundant. Of course, we must remember that in the original manuscripts of the New Testament there were no punctuation marks. There is no other occasion when our Lord used such an expression as "Verily I say unto thee today." (See Matthew 8:10, Mark 13:37.) When anyone uses the present indicative form of the verb he does not need to use the adverb "today," because it is implicit in the tense of the verb. The Lord could not have been speaking to him yesterday; He was speaking at a particular moment and did not need to indicate that moment.

The word "today" is the answer to the thief's request to be remembered when the Lord came into His Kingdom. It was as if the Lord were telling him, "You don't have to wait until I come back into my Kingdom, but you will be with me today as soon as you die. As of today, your spirit, which is going to live on after you die on your cross near me, is going to be with me." There can be no mistaking the meaning of these words of our Lord.

But where did Christ meet this thief after death? The Lord called that place paradise. How can anyone twist the words of Christ to mean that He was speaking about His body and the thief's body meeting each other in the tomb? Of what significance or importance would this be to the thief, to be told that his body, unable to feel or know anything, would meet with the body of

Christ? He knew perfectly well that his body was going to be buried, because the Jews believed in the burial of the body. Therefore Christ's words would convey no news to him. He knew he could not escape physical burial. What was of concern to him was the fate of his spirit or soul.

Christ did not merely promise that when the thief died his body would be buried in paradise, but that his soul would be with Christ in paradise. Nor could paradise be taken to mean a place of nonexistence. Paradise meant a place of conscious enjoyment. It meant the place in *hadees* where the believers had been going until that time. The other thief who did not repent simply went to that place in *hadees* reserved for the spirits of unbelievers. In order for anyone either to enjoy paradise or to feel punishment in *hadees,* however, it is necessary for him to be a conscious being. If the thief who repented could not feel anything in paradise, or the presence of Jesus Christ, then Christ's promise would not have been of any comfort to him.

Another verse that helps us to understand where the center of man's thought lies is I Corinthians 2:11: "For what man knoweth the things of a man, save the spirit of man which is in him?" What enables man to think is not his body or even his material brain, but the spirit, that immaterial entity with which God has imbued him.

It is impossible for a conscious being to

exist without conscious thought. It is therefore possible for man to exist as a conscious entity when his spirit is separated from his body at death. Death kills the material brain of man, but this does not mean it can also kill the ability of man to think as spirit separated from its physical counterpart. Since it is not the body but the spirit that thinks, wills, plans, remembers, and is related to God, it follows that the conscious existence of man after death does not depend upon the body. Man's spirit continues to function separately from the body after death.

What has the Church believed ever since its inception? All the martyrs of the early Church believed that after death they would continue to exist in a conscious state. They endured persecution and martyrdom in the confidence that death would usher them into the presence of the Lord. Not a single martyr of the Apostolic Church had the least doubt about conscious existence after death.

One of these martyrs, Polycarp, a companion of the Apostle John, suffered a martyr's death in A.D. 166, at the age of 87. It is evident from his biography that he had a constant and living faith that once he died he would be in the presence of Christ. This was the doctrine these martyrs were taught directly by the apostles and by the Scriptures.

Anyone who visits the Catacombs of Rome, where the bodies of martyrs were buried during the first three centuries of the Christian era, can see proof of the living hope that possessed these heroes and heroines of the faith. Some of the inscriptions upon their tombs read as follows:

"In Christ, Alexander is not dead, but lives—his body is resting in the grave."

"One who lives with God."

"He went to live with Christ."

"He was taken up into his eternal home."

It is interesting to note that the word "death" is not used even once for these saints of God. Death was followed immediately by glory.

What Is Paradise Like?

We have already seen from the Word of God that the souls of the righteous dead go immediately to paradise. But what is paradise like?

In Philippians 1:22-24 Paul presents life after death as something very much better than this present life. "For I am in a strait betwixt two," he says, "having a desire to depart, and to be with Christ; which is far better" (v. 23). He speaks here of the state of the believer immediately after death as one of conscious enjoyment, with no time lapse at all.

The greatest joy of the believer in paradise is to be in Christ's presence. "And to be with Christ," says Paul. That in itself is paradise. It is the source of indescribable joy. Paul expresses the same assured belief in II Corinthians 5:6-8.

Consider the words of our Lord in His high priestly prayer in John 17:24: "Father, I will that they also, whom thou hast given me, be with me where I am; that they may behold my glory, which thou hast given me: for thou lovedst me before the foundation of the world." Here Christ reveals that when we are with Him in paradise we shall have the opportunity of seeing His glory. Where could we find a greater privilege than this? If we only had a glimpse of the glory of paradise to which the faithful dead have gone, we would never desire their return to earth.

Psalm 16 is a messianic Psalm, that is, one of the many Psalms that refer to the Lord Jesus as the coming Messiah. In verse 11 it says, "In thy presence is fullness of joy; at thy right hand there are pleasures forevermore." Our pleasures and joys on earth are incomplete. It is only in the presence of the Lord that we shall know unalloyed enjoyment. Heaven is a place of great joy, and not the least of the joys of heaven is described in Luke 15:7: "I say unto you, that likewise joy shall be in heaven over one sinner that repenteth, more than over ninety and nine just persons, which need no repentance."

Paradise is a place or state that the human mind finds it impossible adequately to conceive of or describe. Paul was caught up into paradise on one occasion, as he relates in II Corinthians 12:1-4. It was there that he heard "unspeakable words," that is to say, words that man can neither speak nor understand. This indicates that man's life in paradise is vastly different from life on earth. If we had the capacity to understand this heavenly life, no doubt our Lord would have revealed its details to us, and Paul would have tried to give us some idea of it. But neither could find the proper words in our human vocabulary to describe heaven and paradise.

However, God's Word does reveal that it is a state of blessedness. Revelation 14:13 says, "And I heard a voice from heaven saying unto me, Write, Blessed are the dead which die in the Lord from henceforth: Yea, saith the Spirit, that they may rest from their labours; and their works do follow them." From this verse we conclude that the condition to which the blessed and righteous dead pass on is a state of rest. And this rest begins immediately after death, with no time lapse. Of course, we must remember that this verse deals with those who are going to die during the Great Tribulation that shall come upon the earth after the Rapture of the Church of Christ, but it also applies generally to all who die now.

Another verse that shows death to be a blessed state for the believer is Psalm 116:15: "Precious in the sight of the Lord is the death of his saints." Death could hardly be considered precious if it meant nothing but extinction of personality. The death of the believer is precious precisely because it brings him into a closer communion and relationship with Christ. The believer in Christ is liberated from all those restrictions that he endured while in the body on earth. He is no longer buffeted by temptation through the attacks of Satan and his own sinful nature.

In these verses we have God's revelation concerning the state of man after death. We are given no further details. Undoubtedly there is good reason for this. First of all, our state after death—life in paradise—will be so different from our present life in time and space that we could not comprehend any description of it. This does not mean that the Lord could not describe it, but that we are incapable of understanding such a description. Life there is completely spiritual, in a spiritual environment in the realm of the eternal and infinite.

It is also true that, if we could understand how infinitely better life is in heaven compared to life on earth, we would immediately long to go there and thus lose our will or incentive to live one more moment on this earth. Though the Apostle Paul had the privilege of getting a glimpse of heaven, afterward he found it impossible to bring that experience back to total recall, or to explain in human words the heavenly glory that he saw. (See II Corinthians 12:1-4.)

Shall We Be Able to Recognize Each Other in Paradise?

It is only natural to ask such a question, especially if we have suffered the sorrow of losing loved ones — a child, a husband or wife, a mother or father. Our hearts cry out, "Am I ever going to see them again? Am I going to recognize them in heaven?"

What does the Bible have to say on this very important question?

In II Samuel 12:23, David said concerning his child who had died, "Can I bring him back again? I shall go to him, but he shall not return to me." David knew that he, too, would one day go to the land of the dead and meet his son, and that he would recognize him. Otherwise he would not have been able to take comfort from the thought.

Christ said to the thief who was dying on a cross with Him at Calvary, "Verily I say unto thee, to day shalt thou be with me in paradise" (Luke 23:43). Our Lord knew that He would recognize Christ when both met there. Otherwise Christ's words would not have brought him any comfort.

Paul would not have said that he was possessed of such a great desire to go to paradise and be with Christ if he could not be sure of recognizing Christ there. (See Philippians 1:21-24.)

And Christ's disciples recognized Moses and Elijah when they met them on the Mount of Transfiguration. (See Matthew 17:1-8.) If the living disciples could recognize the spirits of Moses and Elijah when they took on visible form and descended to earth, undoubtedly the believers will be able to recognize and identify people in heaven. Though the disciples had never met Moses and Elijah, and were not even introduced to them on this occasion, they knew intuitively who they were. This leads us to believe that the ability of recognition will be much more developed in us there than it is here.

And in the account of the rich man and Lazarus in Luke 16:19-31, we see that the rich man recognized Abraham and Lazarus after his death.

It is evident, therefore, that, since paradise is far better than this earth, we can be sure our knowledge there will not be less than it is here but greater. If we know our loved ones down here on earth, undoubtedly we shall know them more completely up there, in a most profound fellowship of love. As the Apostle Paul tells us in I Corinthians 13:12, "For now we see through a glass, darkly; but then face to face: now I know in part;

but then shall I know even as also I am known."
We conclude, therefore, that we have firm Scriptural grounds for believing we shall be able to recognize our loved ones in heaven or paradise. Furthermore, our heightened ability there will enable us to recognize many others whom we may not have known in the course of history, even as the disciples recognized Moses and Elijah, whom they had never met.

Unrestricted by the limitations of space and time, every believer will have the opportunity of closer fellowship with the Lord in heaven than he enjoys here. There is no doubt that we shall recognize Him even as He recognizes us.

We must stress, however, that the state of the believer in paradise, though far better than his present earthly state, is still imperfect. There is an important event still to take place which will complete his eternal bliss, and that is the resurrection of the body and its reunion with the soul or spirit at Christ's second coming. Therefore all the righteous now in paradise are waiting for their resurrection bodies.

Actually, no righteous person has yet entered into the final and eternal heaven where we shall dwell forever. Nor has any sinner entered into the final and eternal hell, the place of eternal torment. Paradise is not the final heaven, but the place to which the souls or spirits of the righteous ones go at death to be in the presence of Christ. The final heaven will be occupied by the righteous only after the resurrection of their bodies. This marvelous event is described in the last chapters of the book of Revelation. Let us therefore not confuse the final eternal heaven with the present paradise in which the righteous dead dwell until the resurrection day.

The Two Resurrections
of the Dead

Up to this point we have ascertained that the souls or spirits of the righteous dead are in paradise, or the third heaven, where they are waiting for the day of resurrection—that day when their bodies will be rejoined with their spirits, and they will go to the eternal, final heaven to dwell forever. The spirits of the unrighteous dead are now in *hadees,* where they are waiting for their final judgment in hell.

The Bible clearly teaches that the bodies of all the righteous and unrighteous dead will be resurrected and joined to their spirits. In I Corinthians 15 we read the important arguments brought forth by Paul for believing in the resurrection of the bodies of believers as a result of the historic event of Christ's resurrection. (See the author's extensive exposition of this great resurrection chapter in his 869-page book, *Conquering the Fear of Death.)*

God who created our bodies out of nothing, as well as our spirits, and the whole universe, is certainly able to recreate our resurrection bodies with the same characteristics they had on earth. Of course, we do not know the exact composition of these bodies, except that they will be spiritual bodies. (See I Corinthians 15:44.)

The resurrection of the body is also taught in the Old Testament. Consider these two passages:

Job 19:25-27, and especially verse 26: "And though after my skin worms destroy this body, yet in my flesh shall I see God."

Daniel 12:2: "And many of them that sleep in the dust of the earth shall awake, some to everlasting life, and some to shame and everlasting contempt."

Christ also taught the resurrection of the body in John 5:28, 29: "Marvel not at this: for the hour is coming, in the which all that are in the graves shall hear his voice, and shall come forth; they that have done good, unto the resurrection of life; and they that have done evil, unto the resurrection of damnation."

Paul has given us the same teaching in Acts 24:15: "And [we] have hope toward God, which they [the Jews] themselves also allow, that there shall be a resurrection of the dead, both of the just and unjust."

The question immediately arises, Will the resurrection of the righteous and the unrighteous dead occur simultaneously? There are passages in the Bible that tell us there will be two resurrections, occurring at different times.

112

In Revelation 20:6 we read, "Blessed and holy is he that hath part in the first resurrection: on such the second death hath no power, but they shall be priests of God and of Christ, and shall reign with him a thousand years." This is the resurrection of the saints, which will take place before the millennial reign of Christ on earth.

Verse 5 says, "But the rest of the dead," which of course means the unrighteous ones, "lived not again until the thousand years were finished." Therefore, since there is a first resurrection, there is also a second resurrection. The first concerns the saints before the millennial reign of Christ, and the second concerns the unrighteous ones after the millennial reign of Christ on earth.

The Apostle Paul, in Philippians 3:10, 11, voices an aspiration that is not fully brought out by our English translation. He says, "That I may know him, and the power of his resurrection, and the fellowship of his sufferings, being made conformable unto his death; if by any means I might attain unto the resurrection of the dead." What does he mean by the expression, "if by any means I might attain unto the resurrection of the dead"?

The word in the original Greek text is not *anastasis*, which means "resurrection," but the compound word *exsanastasis*, which is made up of the preposition *ex*, meaning "out of," and *anastasis*, meaning "resurrection." If we were to

113

paraphrase it, we could say, "if by any means I manage to escape from the midst of the dead ones."

Paul knows that when the saints are resurrected they will be taken up from the midst of the other dead, leaving the unrighteous dead behind. It is a resurrection that occurs in the midst of the dead, but not for all the dead. This is going to be one of the rewards of the faithful ones.

In I Corinthians 15, Paul deals extensively with the resurrection of the dead. He tells us in verse 23, "But every man in his own order: Christ the firstfruits; afterward they that are Christ's at his coming." Basically the Apostle is dealing here with the resurrection of the believers, not the unbelievers. Therefore he speaks of their resurrection as an event that will take place as a result of the resurrection of Christ—they in their "own order."

Verse 24 tells us, "Then cometh the end." The Greek word for "end" here, *telos,* does not mean "termination," however, but rather "the goal or purpose" of the resurrection of Christ And that goal or purpose is that we may one day also be raised from among the dead. It is for this purpose that Christ rose from the dead, that we might follow suit. This also includes, of course, the resurrection of the unrighteous ones for the purpose of punishing them. As the believers are resurrected for the purpose of rewarding them for their faith in Christ, so the unbelievers are resurrected for the purpose of receiving their due punishment.

In Luke 14:14, our Lord says, "And thou shalt be blessed; for they [that is, the poor on whom the believers showed compassion] cannot recompense thee: for thou shalt be recompensed at the resurrection of the just." Therefore the resurrection of the just is presented as a time of reward for the good deeds of the believers while on earth.

When Will the Resurrection of Believers Take Place? (Part 1)

The Bible reveals that the resurrection of the just will take place when Christ returns for His Church to take her unto Himself. The Apostle Paul very clearly teaches this in I Thessalonians 4:13-17:

"But I would not have you to be ignorant, brethren, concerning them which are asleep, that ye sorrow not, even as others which have no hope. For if we believe that Jesus died and rose again, even so them also which sleep in Jesus will God bring with him. For this we say unto you by the word of the Lord, that we which are alive and remain unto the coming of the Lord shall not prevent [precede] them which are asleep. For the Lord himself shall descend from heaven with a shout, with the voice of the archangel, and with the trump of God: and the dead in Christ shall rise first: then we which are alive and remain shall be caught up together with them in the clouds, to meet the Lord in the air; and so shall we ever be with the Lord."

Paul tells us here that Christ will come

down from heaven bringing with Him the spirits of the righteous ones who are now dwelling in His presence. These spirits will then receive their resurrection bodies, because "the dead in Christ shall rise first." After this takes place, "then we which are alive and remain shall be caught up together with them in the clouds, to meet the Lord in the air: and so shall we ever be with the Lord."

Paul, speaking of this same important event, says in I Corinthians 15:51, 52, "Behold, I shew you a mystery; We shall not all sleep, but we shall all be changed, in a moment, in the twinkling of an eye, at the last trump: for the trumpet shall sound, and the dead shall be raised incorruptible, and we shall be changed." Throughout this whole 15th chapter Paul is speaking of the resurrection of believers. Therefore it is to them alone that these two verses refer. Continuing in the 53rd verse he says, "For this corruptible must put on incorruption, and this mortal must put on immortality." Incorruption and immortality are attributes that refer only to the resurrection bodies of the believers, as we shall see in our next chapter.

And Paul continues: "So when this corruptible shall have put on incorruption, and this mortal shall have put on immortality, then shall be brought to pass the saying that is written, Death is swallowed up in victory" (verse 54). The shouts of victory enunciated by Paul, "O death, where is thy sting? O grave, where is thy victory?" (verse 55), refer only to those who are changed without having tasted death, that is to say, those who will still be alive when the Lord comes to receive His Church unto Himself when He appears for the second time. These are the only ones who will be able to shout, "O death, where is thy sting? O grave, where is thy victory?"

We therefore arrive at the following conclusion: All of us will be changed—both the dead in Christ and those who are alive and belong to Christ when He returns. This will happen at the Rapture of the Church. Both these groups, the resurrected saints and the transformed living saints, will be caught up in the clouds, to meet the Lord in the air and be with Him forever.

However, before these resurrected and transformed believers can enter into the final heaven, there are certain events that must take place. One of these is the judgment of the believers for their works. There is some confusion in regard to this judgment. Some think it will take place immediately after death. Others believe that it will take place at the end of the age, when all men will be judged as to whether they received and rejected Christ, and believers will be judged for their works.

The Bible teaches that God's judgment concerning the eternal destiny of people takes place down here on earth, and is fixed at the moment of death. Whether a man is going to enjoy eternal bliss in the presence of the Lord or suffer eternally in hell is determined by his decision to receive or reject Christ. His eternal destiny, therefore, is determined right here on earth. He reaps what he sows.

In Romans 8:1 Paul says, "There is therefore now no condemnation to them which are in Christ Jesus, who walk not after the flesh, but after the Spirit." Christ said the same thing in John 5:24, "Verily, verily, I say unto you, He that heareth my word, and believeth on him that sent me, hath everlasting life, and shall not come into condemnation; but is passed from death unto life."

Therefore the judgment of the believer, that is, as to whether his sin has been blotted out and forgiven, is determined the very moment a person believes in Christ. The judgment of sin has really taken place on the cross of Christ, as the following verses indicate:

Galatians 3:13: "Christ hath redeemed us from the curse of the law, being made a curse for us; for it is written, Cursed is every one that hangeth on a tree."

I Peter 2:24: "Who his own self bare our sins in his own body on the tree, that we, being dead to sins, should live unto righteousness: by whose stripes ye were healed."

II Corinthians 5:21: "For he hath made him to be sin for us, who [that is, Christ] knew no sin;

119

that we might be made the righteousness of God in him."

The sins of the believers have already been judged and cast out. Paul says in I Timothy 5:24, "Some men's sins are open beforehand, going before to judgment; and some men they follow after." But speaking of believers he says in verse 25 that they will be judged only as far as their good works are concerned, works that they did, not for the purpose of obtaining salvation, but as fruits of their faith in Christ. "Likewise also the good works of some are manifest beforehand; and they that are otherwise cannot be hid."

The born-again person will not be judged for his sins, because these have already been judged in the person of the Lord Jesus Christ on the cross. He will be judged, however, for the works of his Christian life and faith. This will take place after the dead in Christ are resurrected and the living believers are changed.

In II Corinthians 5:10 Paul says, "For we must all appear before the judgment seat of Christ; that every one may receive the things done in his body, according to that he hath done, whether it be good or bad." Here Paul is not referring to all men, but only to believers. And in I Corinthians 3:13 he says, "Every man's work shall be made manifest: for the day shall declare it, because it shall be revealed by fire; and the fire shall try every man's work of what sort it is."

Therefore, this appearing before the judgment seat of Christ is for the believers, to assess their work of faith and reward them accordingly. This judgment will take place when the Lord returns, as Paul tells us in I Corinthians 4:5: "Therefore judge nothing before the time, until the Lord come, who both will bring to light the hidden things of darkness, and will make manifest the counsels of the hearts: and then shall every man have praise of God." The praise and reward is exclusively for the children of God, the born-again believers, and not for the unrighteous.

The Bible refers to various crowns that will be given to believers during this day of judgment for their works. In James 1:12, for instance, we read about the crown of life: "Blessed is the man that endureth temptation: for when he is tried, he shall receive the crown of life, which the Lord hath promised to them that love him." The same promise occurs in Revelation 2:10: "Fear none of those things which thou shalt suffer: behold, the devil shall cast some of you into prison, that ye may be tried; and ye shall have tribulation ten days: be thou faithful unto death, and I will give thee a crown of life."

Another reward spoken of is the crown of glory in I Peter 5:2-4: "Feed the flock of God which is among you, taking the oversight thereof, not by constraint, but willingly; not for filthy lucre, but of a ready mind; neither as being lords over God's heritage, but being ensamples to the flock. And when the chief Shepherd shall appear, ye shall receive a crown of glory that fadeth not away."

Also in I Thessalonians 2:19 we read of the crown of rejoicing: "For what is our hope, or joy or crown of rejoicing? Are not even ye in the presence of our Lord Jesus Christ at his coming?"

We also have the crown of righteousness, which is mentioned in II Timothy 4:8: "Henceforth there is laid up for me a crown of righteousness, which the Lord, the righteous judge, shall give me at that day; and not to me only, but unto all them also that love his appearing."

Again, in I Corinthians 9:25-27, Paul speaks of an incorruptible crown: "And every man that striveth for the mastery is temperate in all things. Now they do it to obtain a corruptible crown; but we an incorruptible. I therefore so run, not as uncertainly; so fight I, not as one that beateth the air: but I keep under my body, and bring it into subjection: lest that by any means, when I have preached to others, I myself should be a castaway."

When Will the Resurrection of Believers Take Place? (Part 2)

We have seen that, at the *parousia* or appearance of the Lord, those who are dead in Christ will rise, and those who are alive in Christ will be changed, so that all together they appear before the judgment seat of Christ to be judged for their earthly works and receive the rewards they deserve, and which the Lord wants to bestow on them because of His mercy and sovereignty.

However, there are further events that will take place before the righteous enter upon their final heavenly existence. One is that great event of "the marriage of the Lamb" (Jesus Christ), mentioned in Revelation 19:7-9: "Let us be glad and rejoice, and give honour to him: for the marriage of the Lamb is come, and his wife hath made herself ready. And to her was granted that she should be arrayed in fine linen, clean and white: for the fine linen is the righteousness of saints. And he saith unto me, Write, Blessed are they which are called unto the marriage supper of the Lamb. And he saith unto me, These are the true sayings of God."

The woman or the bride of Christ will be His true Church, made up of all born-again children of God from all races and tongues. At this particular moment, this bride of Christ, His Church, will be made up of the dead believers whose bodies will have been resurrected, and the believers in Christ whom He will find alive and whose bodies will be changed.

Another event is the Great Tribulation that will come upon the earth during the period when the faithful ones will be judged for their works and the wedding of the Lamb takes place in heaven. This period of the Great Tribulation will be terminated by the "revelation" of Christ.

These two phases of the second coming of Christ are distinguished in the Word of God. One of them is called the *parousia,* which will be the personal appearance of Christ for His saints, at which time the dead in Christ will be raised and those who are in Christ and still alive will be changed. For the most part, but not exclusively, the second phase of Christ's coming is called *apokalupsis* or revelation, when Christ shall come with His saints. This will take place after the judgment of the believers' works and the wedding of the Lamb.

In the following verses the word *parousia* is used to indicate the first phase of the coming of the Lord to take up His Church: "And as he sat upon the mount of Olives, the disciples came unto him privately, saying, Tell us, when shall these things be? and what shall be the sign of thy coming [*parousia,*] and of the end of the world [aeon or age]?'' (Matthew 24:3). And in verse 27 of the same chapter we read: "For as the lightning cometh out of the east, and shineth even unto the west; so shall also the coming [*parousia*] of the Son of man be." And in verse 37 we read: "But as the days of Noe [Noah] were, so shall also the coming [*parousia*] of the Son of man be." And verse 39 says: "And [they] knew not until the flood came, and took them all away; so shall also the coming [*parousia*] of the Son of man be."

Here are other Scriptures in which the word *parousia* is mentioned:

I Corinthians 15:23: "But every man in his own order: Christ the firstfruits; afterward they that are Christ's at his coming [*parousia*]."

I Thessalonians 2:19: "For what is our hope, or joy, or crown of rejoicing? Are not even ye in the presence of our Lord Jesus Christ at his coming [*parousia*]?"

I Thessalonians 4:15: "For this we say unto you by the word of the Lord, that we which are alive and remain unto the coming [*parousia*] of the Lord shall not prevent [precede] them which are asleep."

I Thessalonians 5:23: "And the very God of peace sanctify you wholly; and I pray God your whole spirit and soul and body be preserved blameless unto the coming [*parousia*] of our Lord

125

Jesus Christ."

II Thessalonians 2:1, 2: "Now we beseech you, brethren, by the coming [*parousia*] of our Lord Jesus Christ, and by our gathering together unto him, that ye be not soon shaken in mind, or be troubled, neither by spirit, nor by word, nor by letter as from us, as that the day of Christ is at hand."

There are other verses that refer to the *parousia* of the Lord, such as Luke 17:34-36, John 14:3, etc.

Verses that use the word *apokalupsis* are:

Revelation 1:1: "The revelation [*apokalupsis*] of Jesus Christ, which God gave unto him, to shew unto his servants things which must shortly come to pass; and he sent and signified it by his angel unto his servant John." And then later, in verse 7, He tells us what this is all about: "Behold, he cometh with clouds; and every eye shall see him, and they also which pierced him: and all kindreds of the earth shall wail because of him. Even so, Amen." Here it is evident that even the enemies of Christ will see Him during His "revelation."

Colossians 3:4: Although this verse does not contain the word *apokalupsis,* "revelation," we find the Greek verb *phaneroothee,* "shall appear," which for all practical purposes means the same thing. "When Christ, who is our life, shall appear, then shall ye also appear with him in glory." Please observe here that Christ appears or is revealed in glory with His saints.

Jude 14: This verse also tells us about the coming of the Lord with His saints. "Behold, the Lord cometh with ten thousands of his saints."

Zechariah 14:5: "And ye shall flee to the valley of the mountains; for the valley of the mountains shall reach unto Azal: yea, ye shall flee, like as ye fled from before the earthquake in the days of Uzziah king of Judah: and the Lord my God shall come, and all the saints with thee."

II Thessalonians 1:7, 8: "And to you who are troubled rest with us, when the Lord Jesus shall be revealed from heaven with his mighty angels, in flaming fire taking vengeance on them that know not God, and that obey not the gospel of our Lord Jesus Christ."

This *apokalupsis* or "revelation" of Christ, that is, His coming with His saints, will be the termination of the Great Tribulation period, which will usher in the millennial Kingdom of Christ upon this earth with His saints, as we see in Revelation 20:6: "Blessed and holy is he that hath part in the first resurrection: on such the second death hath no power, but they shall be priests of God and of Christ, and shall reign with him a thousand years."

After this, the earth will be renewed with fire, as we are told in II Peter 3:10-13: "But the day of the Lord will come as a thief in the night; in the which the heavens shall pass away with a great noise, and the elements shall melt with fervent heat, the earth also and the works that are therein shall be burned up. Seeing then that all these things shall be dissolved, what manner of persons ought ye to be in all holy conversation [manner of living] and godliness, looking for and hasting unto the coming of the day of God, wherein the heavens being on fire shall be dissolved, and the elements shall melt with fervent heat? Nevertheless we, according to his promise, look for new heavens and a new earth, wherein dwelleth righteousness."

With the renewal of the earth by fire, as Peter informs us, there shall come down from heaven a new Jerusalem which is the eternal habitation of the saints, as we read in Revelation 21:1, 2: "And I saw a new heaven and a new earth: for the first heaven and the first earth were passed away; and there was no more sea. And I John saw the holy city, new Jerusalem, coming down from God out of heaven, prepared as a bride adorned for her husband."

The Resurrection Body, Similar Yet Different

Before we examine what the Bible has to say about the final and eternal heaven that will be the dwelling place of the faithful, it will be helpful to see what it reveals about our resurrection body.

In the first place, this body will not be exactly the same as the one that was placed in the grave. In I Corinthians 15:37 the Apostle Paul declares, "And that which thou sowest, thou sowest not that body that shall be, but bare grain, it may chance of wheat, or of some other grain." The plant that springs up from the ground is different from the seed that was planted. Similarly the resurrection body will be different from our present body. And yet there will be a similarity; as the seed so will the plant be. A corn kernel will produce a cornstalk.

There is no doubt that the resurrection body will be far superior to our present body, and yet it will be recognizable as the same body. Our loved ones will know who we are. The distinctiveness of its personality will be preserved. This does not mean that its substance will be the same as that of our present body. It will be entirely new, but will maintain the recognizable characteristics of our personality as presently constituted.

In I Corinthians 15:35 Paul propounds a question that concerns all of us. He says, "But some man will say, How are the dead raised up? and with what body do they come?" And he goes on to answer his question in verses 36, 37, and 42: "Thou fool, that which thou sowest is not quickened [made alive] except it die: and that which thou sowest, thou sowest not that body that shall be, but bare grain, it may chance of wheat, or of some other grain. . . . So also is the resurrection of the dead. It is sown in corruption; it is raised in incorruption." In spite of the fact that our present body is planted in the ground as a corruptible body, it will be raised incorruptible. This means that it will no longer be subject to deterioration.

Then in verses 53 and 54 he tells us, "For this corruptible must put on incorruption, and this mortal must put on immortality. So when this corruptible shall have put on incorruption, and this mortal shall have put on immortality, then shall be brought to pass the saying that is written, Death is swallowed up in victory."

Paul speaks about our body as the one that is going to be resurrected, even as the body of Christ was resurrected. He tells us that it will be incorruptible and immortal. We know what incor-

130

ruptible means: it will no longer be subject to a breakdown into the elements of which it is made. And it will be immortal, that is to say, no longer separated from our spirit as it was at death. When Adam sinned, God imposed a double punishment: for his soul, spiritual death (separation of man's spirit from God's Spirit); and for his body, material death—that is, Adam's body become mortal, so that at death it would be separated from his spirit. This bodily mortality was passed on through Adam to every man, as Paul tells us in Romans 5:12: "Wherefore, as by one man sin entered into the world, and death by sin; and so death passed upon all men, for that all have sinned." Our body dies as a result of Adam's sin and disobedience. This curse, however, will no longer affect our resurrection body. In reality, only Christ is now said to possess immortality, as Paul says in I Timothy 6:16: "Who only hath immortality, dwelling in the light which no man can approach unto; whom no man hath seen, nor can see: to whom be honour and power everlasting. Amen."

Here some clarification is needed as to the meaning of eternal life. Not all people possess this; only those who have received Jesus Christ as their Saviour. That's what He tells us in John 5:24: "Verily, verily, I say unto you, He that heareth my word, and believeth on him that sent me, hath everlasting life, and shall not come into condemnation [judgment]; but is passed from

131

death unto life." Eternal life is a gift that man receives by faith from Jesus Christ.

All men, however, whether righteous or not, continue to have a conscious existence after death.

In discussing immortality we need to recognize two things: 1) The Bible teaches that immortality is a gift that God confers only on those who have received eternal life by faith in Christ Jesus; and, 2) The faithful dead do not possess this immortality now, but will receive it when their bodies are raised at the *parousia* or coming of the Lord. The immortality, therefore, of which the Bible speaks does not pertain to the soul of man but to the body of the believer. The Bible considers man's body, whether that of a believer or an unbeliever, as mortal; and it declares that the Lord Jesus Christ, as God, is the only One who possesses immortality (I Timothy 6:16).

The following verses show that man's body is mortal:

I Corinthians 15:54: "So when this corruptible shall have put on incorruption, and this mortal shall have put on immortality, then shall be brought to pass the saying that is written, Death is swallowed up in victory."

Romans 6:12: "Let not sin therefore reign in your mortal body, that ye should obey it in the lusts thereof."

Romans 8:11: "But if the Spirit of him that raised up Jesus from the dead dwell in you, he that raised up Christ from the dead shall also quicken [give life to] your mortal bodies by his Spirit that dwelleth in you."

The Jehovah's Witnesses try to accuse those who rightly divide the Word of Truth of believing that man is immortal now. We believe no such thing. We believe the Bible teaching that man is now mortal. This means that his body is mortal and dies, but his soul lives on. Physical death does not affect the personal existence of the soul. When Scripture speaks of death in connection with the soul, it means spiritual death, the separation of man's spirit from God's Spirit.

Therefore we must not thoughtlessly say that man is immortal. The soul of man does not cease to exist after death as a spiritual entity, but man's body ceases to exist as the dwelling place of the soul. The day will come, however, when the body of the believer will be clothed with immortality which God will give him. In other words, as his soul is now, so will his body become incorruptible and immortal.

Further Proof That
the Righteous Dead
Are in Heaven

Our conclusion so far has been that the resurrection bodies of believers will be incorruptible and immortal. That's what Paul teaches in I Corinthians 15:42 and 53: "So also is the resurrection of the dead. It is sown in corruption; it is raised in incorruption. . . . For this corruptible must put on incorruption, and this mortal must put on immortality." We know that these verses refer only to the body, for the Bible teaches that the soul or spirit returns to God when man dies. Since God dwells "in the heavens" (Psalm 123:1), that is where the believer's spirit goes at death.

True, we don't have any direct statement that the believer's spirit goes to heaven at death, but this is implicit in the New Testament. When Stephen, the first Christian martyr, was dying, he called upon Christ who was and is in the heavens to receive his spirit (Acts 7:59). In Philippians 1:23 Paul expressed a desire to depart from this world and to be with Christ, "which is far better." Thus we conclude that the place of joy and rest, heaven or paradise, is situated above, while *hadees* is situated below. That is what the Bible states, although we cannot pinpoint exactly what is meant by "the lower parts of the earth" (Ephesians 4:9).

Some people theorize that when Christ died He descended into *hadees,* where He joined the righteous dead of the Old Testament who were somehow kept prisoners there. Then on His resurrection He liberated them and carried them from *hadees* to the heavens, to which the spirits of believers have gone ever since. They base this theory on Ephesians 4:8-10, which says: "Wherefore he saith, When he ascended up on high, he led captivity captive, and gave gifts unto men. (Now that he ascended, what is it but that he also descended first into the lower parts of the earth? He that descended is the same also that ascended up far above all heavens, that he might fill all things.)"

Such a theory or interpretation does not have the support of any other portion of Scripture. We must take these verses in their context in order to determine their meaning. In Ephesians 4:7-16 Paul discusses the gifts Christ has given to His Church, and the ministering organs that He uses for the upbuilding of His body. Christ gave gifts to men through His Holy Spirit, according to John 16:7, 13, 14 and Acts 2:33. We believe it is these gifts that Paul tells us Christ led captive, or simply captured, and made them His undeniable possession through the victory of the cross and the triumph of His resurrection and ascension to heaven. This captivity did not take place in *hadees* to which He descended, but in the heights of heaven when He entered there as a victor.

This is why the Apostle Paul says, "When he ascended up on high, he led captivity captive, and gave gifts unto men." The gifts of the Holy Spirit were what the victorious Christ captivated, for it is of these gifts that Ephesians 4:7-16 speaks. That is why Peter on the day of Pentecost said, "Therefore being by the right hand of God exalted, and having received of the Father the promise of the Holy Ghost, he hath shed forth this, which ye now see and hear" (Acts 2:33).

For this reason, we cannot find any basis for interpreting Ephesians 4:8-10 as meaning that Christ transferred the faithful dead from *hadees* to paradise or heaven. We do not exclude the possibility of this, but we find no clear revelation of it. At least this passage does not make this matter clear. Although this theory and interpretation are very popular, we cannot in all honesty, in the interests of sound Biblical exegesis, accept it as valid.

During the present new order of the full proclamation of God's grace initiated by Christ's resurrection and ascension to heaven, when those who believe in Christ die, their spirits no longer go to *hadees* but are in the presence of the

136

Lord in the heavens (Hebrews 12:23). The instances we have previously cited of Stephen and the Apostle Paul clearly affirm that when the righteous die they go to be with Christ; and we know that Christ is not now in *hadees* but in heaven.

That Christ would not remain in *hadees* was prophesied by David in Psalm 16:10: "For thou wilt not leave my soul in hell; neither wilt thou suffer thine Holy One to see corruption." Christ's resurrection was the fulfillment of this prophecy according to Acts 2:27 and 31.

Christ's ascension was prophesied by David in Psalm 68:18: "Thou hast ascended on high, thou hast led captivity captive: thou hast received gifts for men." Take this in conjunction with Ephesians 4:8.

Here are other verses that refer to Christ's ascension to heaven:

Mark 16:19: "So then after the Lord had spoken unto them, he was received up into heaven, and sat on the right hand of God."

Luke 24:51: "And it came to pass, while he blessed them, he was parted from them, and carried up into heaven."

Acts 1:9: "And when he had spoken these things, while they beheld, he was taken up; and a cloud received him out of their sight."

Hebrews 4:14: "Seeing then that we have a great high priest, that is passed into the heavens, Jesus the Son of God. . . ."

I Peter 3:22: "Who is gone into heaven, and is on the right hand of God; angels and authorities and powers being made subject unto him."

See also Hebrews 8:1; 9:24; 7:25, and Acts 7:55-60.

From these verses it is an incontrovertible fact that when Christ ascended He went to heaven. But what about the righteous dead? One of my radio listeners wrote to me asking, "Where in the Bible does it say that when the believer dies he goes to heaven?" My answer was that although the New Testament does not say it in those words, this truth is implicit throughout its pages. Since it declares that, when the believer dies, he goes to be with Christ—and since Christ is in heaven—we logically conclude that the believer goes to heaven also. Paul conclusively taught that when the believer is absent from the body he is present with the Lord (Philippians 1:23 and II Corinthians 5:6-8). And where is that but heaven?

Ever since the time when Christ descended into *hadees* and then rose from the dead, *hadees* has ceased to include paradise or Abraham's bosom (Luke 16:22). During His earthly ministry Christ referred to *hadees* as His future enemy and that of His followers. In speaking to Peter about the persecution Christ's Church would have to suffer, He assured him that *hadees* would not be able to prevail against it.

"And I say also unto thee, That thou art Peter, and upon this rock I will build my church; and the gates of hell [*hadees*] shall not prevail against it." The rock upon which Christ's Church was going to be built was Peter's confession that he had just made, "Thou art the Christ, the Son of the living God" (Matthew 16:16).

Therefore, if *hadees* is to be the enemy of the Church, how can it still contain that section to which the righteous went, still go, and will go? After Christ left it, *hadees* or *sheol* became the exclusive destination of the unrighteous dead, instead of the abode of both unrighteous and righteous. Of course, we must not forget that while the righteous were in *hadees* they were being comforted, and were separated from the unrighteous who were in torment.

We must be careful not to go beyond the Scriptural teaching regarding these truths. What is clear, however, is that after the redemption wrought by Christ, the faithful dead go to heaven to be with Him. Through the sacrifice of Christ, the sins of the righteous ones of Old Testament times were paid for and blotted out. And now they are dwelling in the presence of the Lord in the same manner as all who have repented and been forgiven during the New Testament dispensation, as they leave this present earth.

But the unrighteous in this new order like the unrighteous under the old order, go to the same place of torment, called *sheol* or *hadees*.

139

During the judgment of the Great White Throne, *hadees* will be cast into the lake of fire. Revelation 20:14 says, "And death and hell were cast into the lake of fire." This proves that it is now the exclusive abode of the unrighteous, for if the faithful were still there, how could it be possible for them to be cast into the lake of fire?

We can rejoice that the spirits of the righteous dead are now with Christ in paradise or the third heaven.

Where Is Heaven, and Who Is There?

The Bible mentions three heavens:

1) The atmospheric heaven, the heaven of the clouds from which the rain comes down. Acts 14:17 says, "And [God] gave us rain from heaven, and fruitful seasons."

2) The heaven where evil spirits dwell, the kingdom of Satan. Paul speaks of this in Ephesians 6:12: "For we wrestle not against flesh and blood, but against principalities, against powers, against the rulers of the darkness of this world, against spiritual wickedness in high places" (or as the Greek text says, "in the heavens"). Of course, we are not to imagine that this heaven has a physical substance. Since it is the dwelling place of evil spirits, it must be of a spiritual nature.

3) The heaven of heavens, or the third heaven—the dwelling place of God and the site of His throne. "Thou, even thou, art Lord alone; thou hast made heaven, the heaven of heavens, with all their host, the earth, and all things that are therein" (Nehemiah 9:6). "We have such an

high priest, who is set on the right hand of the throne of the Majesty in the heavens" (Hebrews 8:1). In II Corinthians 12:2 and 4 Paul calls this the "third heaven" and "paradise." This is the heaven in which there is great joy over a repenting sinner (Luke 15:7).

Later in our study we shall see that *hadees* for the unrighteous, and paradise for the righteous, are not the final states for men. Eventually there will be hell for the unrighteous and the final heaven or the New Jerusalem for the righteous.

The Jehovah's Witnesses do not believe that, in the Christian dispensation, the righteous dead go to heaven or into the presence of the Lord. They cite the following verses in support of their position:

John 3:13: "And no man hath ascended up to heaven, but he that came down from heaven, even the Son of man which is in heaven."

In order to understand this verse, we must examine it carefully in its proper context. In John 3:10-13 we see that Christ was talking to Nicodemus about the knowledge of heavenly things that people cannot understand, since they cannot even understand earthly phenomena. In regard to heavenly truths our Lord says, "And no man hath ascended up to heaven, but he that came down from heaven, even the Son of man who is in heaven."

In other words, no one ever went up to heaven for the purpose of learning and declaring

142

to men the things he had seen there. The only one capable of speaking about these things is the Son of man who descended from heaven for the specific purpose of declaring heavenly truths.

The Scripture speaks of at least one man, Elijah, who "went up by a whirlwind into heaven" (II Kings 2:11). Undoubtedly Christ was not ignorant of this event, so he could not have merely been saying that no one ever ascended into heaven. What He meant was that no one had ascended into heaven and come down again for the specific purpose of explaining on earth what he had seen in heaven. Only Christ had done this.

We have a similar statement in connection with Enoch: "And Enoch walked with God: and he was not; for God took him" (Genesis 5:24). "By faith Enoch was translated that he should not see death; and was not found, because God had translated him: for before his translation he had this testimony, that he pleased God" (Hebrews 11:5). Enoch was taken into heaven, but he did not go there in order to come down again to declare what he had seen, nor did he ascend bodily on his own power, as Christ did. Our Lord was the only one who did this.

In view of all this, we must reject the claim of the Jehovah's Witnesses that John 3:13 means that born-again Christians do not go to heaven at death.

Another verse the Johovah's Witnesses cite

is Acts 2:34: "For David is not ascended into the heavens: but he saith himself, The Lord said unto my Lord, Sit thou on my right hand." If we accept the theory that Christ transferred the faithful ones of the Old Testament from *hadees* to heaven, then David had already ascended into heaven when Peter was preaching on the day of Pentecost, because Christ had already risen and ascended into heaven.

The true meaning of this verse, then, is that Christ rose from the dead and ascended into heaven in His resurrection body. But David, either found in *hadees,* or according to the transfer theory transferred to heaven with Christ, had not risen physically from the dead so that he could ascend to heaven with an incorruptible and immortal body.

In this sense, then, of course David had not ascended to heaven. Only Christ who rose from the dead had ascended to heaven with a resurrection body.

Thus the subject of Acts 2:34 is not where David is now, but that David had not yet risen from the dead physically, in a resurrection body, and in that sense only had not ascended to heaven; whereas this had taken place in the case of the Lord Jesus Christ.

Characteristics of
the Resurrection Body

In addition to incorruptibility and immortality, the Apostle Paul tells us several other characteristics of the body that believers will receive at the resurrection when Christ comes again.

1) It will be a glorious body in comparison to our present one. "It is sown in dishonour; it is raised in glory" (I Corinthians 15:43a).

2) It will be a power-filled body. "It is sown in weakness; it is raised in power" (43b). What is so weak as a dead body? Yet if Christ dwelt in that body, that is, if the person had received Christ as Saviour during his lifetime, God is going to raise it in power.

3) It will be a spiritual body. "It is sown a natural body; it is raised a spiritual body." Of course, we don't know exactly what that implies. But undoubtedly it will be a body similar to our present one, which will have certain physical feelings, but without our present limitations and restrictions. One main difference will be that it will no longer have a tendency to obey our

145

natural instincts, but only our spiritual ones.

4) It will be similar to Christ's resurrection body, having the same characteristics. "For our conversation is in heaven; from whence also we look for the Saviour, the Lord Jesus Christ: who shall change our vile body, that it may be fashioned like unto his glorious body, according to the working whereby he is able even to subdue all things unto himself" (Philippians 3:20, 21).

John makes a similar statement in I John 3:2: "Beloved, now are we the sons of God, and it doth not yet appear what we shall be: but we know that, when he shall appear, we shall be like him; for we shall see him as he is."

The Psalmist also says, "As for me, I will behold thy face in righteousness: I shall be satisfied, when I awake, with thy likeness" (Psalm 17:15).

This assurance should fill us with great joy. Just to think that our bodies will be similar to Christ's resurrection body is enough to dispel all fear of death.

But if our bodies are going to be like Christ's, let's examine what Scripture has to tell us about the characteristics of His resurrection body.

1) It was a real body, with the same recognizable features as the body He had before His resurrection. He could be seen and touched. And yet His body could go through closed doors and overcome physical distances. No physical restric-

146

tions could stand in its way. Christ made ten appearances with His resurrection body, but let us look at just three instances to prove that His body was real and could be apparent to human touch.

Matthew 28:9: "And as they went to tell his disciples, behold, Jesus met them, saying, All hail. And they came and held him by the feet, and worshipped him."

Luke 24:39: "Behold my hands and my feet, that it is I myself: handle me, and see; for a spirit hath not flesh and bones, as ye see me have."

John 20:26, 27: "And after eight days again his disciples were within, and Thomas with them: then came Jesus, the doors being shut, and stood in the midst, and said, Peace be unto you. Then saith he to Thomas, Reach hither thy finger, and behold my hands; and reach hither thy hand, and thrust it into my side: and be not faithless, but believing."

In John 20:16, 18, Mary Magdalene recognized the Lord, which persuades us that His body after the resurrection was similar to His previous body. His disciples also recognized Him. "And when he had so said, he shewed unto them his hands and his side. Then were the disciples glad, when they saw the Lord" (John 20:20). This is further proof that we shall be able to recognize each other when we are clothed in our glorious resurrection bodies.

2) It was a bloodless body, a body of flesh and bones only. In Luke 24:39 our Lord said, "Behold my hands and my feet, that it is I myself: handle me, and see; for a spirit hath not flesh and bones, as ye see me have." This leads us to conclude that our resurrection bodies will not be of "flesh and blood," because the Word of God tells us "that flesh and blood cannot inherit the kingdom of God" (I Corinthians 15:50). They will be of "flesh and bones," like our Lord's resurrection body. Why will our bodies be bloodless? The purpose of blood in our present bodies is to maintain the constantly weakening cells that are in need of the life of the blood. But where the cells do not deteriorate, because the resurrection body will be incorruptible, there is no need for blood.

In heaven, Scripture indicates that we shall neither eat nor drink; that there will be no sickness, death, or night there. "They shall not hunger or thirst; neither shall the heat nor sun smite them: for he that hath mercy on them shall lead them" (Isaiah 49:10). "And the gates of it shall not be shut at all by day: for there shall be no night there" (Revelation 21:25). "And there shall be no night there; and they need no candle, neither light of the sun; for the Lord God giveth them light: and they shall reign for ever and ever" (Revelation 22:5).

We conclude therefore that we shall not need food, because the purpose of food is to

148

maintain and restore strength to our weak body. Nor will there be sickness, since our body will be incorruptible. Nor will there be any night, for the night is for sleeping, to rest the tired body. Our resurrection body will therefore have no need of nourishment, rest, or sleep.

Our resurrection body will not be subject to death, for it will be incorruptible and immortal. This brings to mind the words of Christ, "Neither can they die any more: for they are equal unto the angels; and are the children of God, being the children of the resurrection" (Luke 20:36). And in Revelation 22:5 we have seen that the believers "shall reign for ever and ever," again a guarantee against death.

To sum it all up, God's Word reveals that the resurrection body will be incorruptible, immortal, glorious, strong, and spiritual; that it will be similar to Christ's glorious resurrection body—a body that can be touched, that does not consist of "flesh and blood" but of "flesh and bones," and that is no longer subject to death.

So far we have only been considering the resurrection body of those who will have died before our Lord returns from heaven to receive His Church to Himself. But what about the bodies of those believers who are still living when He returns? The Apostle Paul tells us about this in I Corinthians 15:51, 52: "Behold, I shew you a mystery; We shall not all sleep, but we shall all be changed, in a moment, in the twinkling of an eye, at the last trump." This indicates that all believers are not going to die before they receive their new bodies. Those who are still alive when the Lord comes for His saints will be transformed.

Of course, *all* believers will be transformed, both the dead and the living, when Christ comes. Paul refers to dead believers in verse 53 when he says, "For this corruptible must put on incorruption," and to the living believers when he says, "and this mortal must put on immortality." Although the bodies of the dead believers will have been corrupted, and must therefore put on incorruption, the bodies of the living, which have not undergone corruption, will be clothed with immortality.

And since there will be no blood in the resurrection body of the dead, there will have to be a similar change in the body of the believers who are alive when the Lord comes. The bodies of both classes of believers will be exactly the same.

The Final Heaven—
What It Will Be Like

So far we have seen that the spirits of believers at death go to paradise or the third heaven, and that at the coming of the Lord their bodies will be raised from the earth to be united with their spirits. We have also seen that the faithful in Christ who are still alive will be transformed. Only then will the believers be in a position to enter the eternal heaven. No saint or believer has entered as yet into the final heaven, and no sinner has entered into the final hell.

In the 4th chapter of the Revelation, as well as in the final chapters, we have a description of the final future heaven. We must not confuse this with the present paradise or heaven which the Bible calls the third heaven, to which the disembodied spirits of believers now go.

Since we have already seen what Scripture has to say about paradise or the third heaven, let's go on to study the Scriptural teaching about the final heaven.

The Bible speaks of it as a city that the Lord

has prepared for the believers. "But now they desire a better country, that is, an heavenly: wherefore God is not ashamed to be called their God: for he hath prepared for them a city" (Hebrews 11:16). "For here we have no continuing city, but we seek one to come" (Hebrews 13:14). We find a description of this city in Revelation 21. In verse 2 it is called "the holy city" and "new Jerusalem." This brings to mind the words of our Lord in John 14:2: "In my Father's house are many mansions: if it were not so, I would have told you. I go to prepare a place for you."

The eternal heaven is also called a country. "For they that say such things declare plainly that they seek a country" (Hebrews 11:14). "But now they desire a better country, that is, an heavenly" (Hebrews 11:16).

The Apostle Peter refers to this final heaven as the place where we shall receive our inheritance. "Blessed be the God and Father of our Lord Jesus Christ, which according to his abundant mercy hath begotten us again unto a lively hope by the resurrection of Jesus Christ from the dead, to an inheritance incorruptible, and undefiled, and that fadeth not away, reserved in heaven for you, who are kept by the power of God through faith unto salvation ready to be revealed in the last time" (I Peter 1:3-5).

This inheritance of the saints will be so great that the Apostle Paul cries out, "Eye hath not seen, nor ear heard, neither have entered into the heart of man, the things which God hath prepared for them that love him" (I Corinthians 2:9). This is why we are advised, "Set your affection on things above, not on things on the earth" (Colossians 3:2).

Therefore, as we look forward to such a country, let us acknowledge the wisdom of what our Lord told us to do in Matthew 6:19, 20: "Lay not up for yourselves treasures upon earth, where moth and rust doth corrupt, and where thieves break through and steal: but lay up for yourselves treasures in heaven, where neither moth nor rust doth corrupt, and where thieves do not break through nor steal." How much better our heavenly country will be than our present country.

Describing the coming eternal heaven, John says in Revelation 21:1-5: "And I saw a new heaven and a new earth: for the first heaven and the first earth were passed away; and there was no more sea. And I John saw the holy city, new Jerusalem, coming down from God out of heaven, prepared as a bride adorned for her husband. And I heard a great voice out of heaven saying, Behold, the tabernacle of God is with men, and he will dwell with them, and they shall be his people, and God himself shall be with them, and be their God. And God shall wipe away all tears from their eyes; and there shall be no more death, neither sorrow, nor crying, neither shall there be any more pain: for the former things are passed away. And he that sat upon the throne said, Behold, I make all things new. And he said unto me, Write: for these words are true and faithful."

In order to give us a faint idea of the glory and brilliance of heaven, John speaks of it in Revelation 21:11 as "Having the glory of God: and her light was like unto a stone most precious, even like a jasper stone, clear as crystal." And using earthly language in an attempt to describe something immeasurably higher and heavenly, he says in verses 21-23, "And the twelve gates were twelve pearls: every several gate was one of pearl: and the street of the city was pure gold, as it were transparent glass. And I saw no temple therein: for the Lord God Almighty and the Lamb are the temple of it. And the city had no need of the sun, neither of the moon, to shine in it: for the glory of God did lighten it, and the Lamb is the light thereof."

Speaking of the purity of heaven, John says in verse 27, "And there shall in no wise enter into it any thing that defileth, neither whatsoever worketh abomination, or maketh a lie: but they which are written in the Lamb's book of life."

And again, in Revelation 22:3-5 he says, "And there shall be no more curse: but the throne of God and of the Lamb shall be in it; and his servants shall serve him: and they shall see his face; and his name shall be in their foreheads.

And there shall be no light of the sun; for the Lord giveth them light: and they shall reign for ever and ever.''

This final heaven will be a place of great rejoicing, because there we shall be in continuous and unhindered touch with God Himself. Where our Lord is, there is heaven. All the other descriptions are merely a shadow before the glory of the presence of the Lord.

It can reasonably be deduced that, since we shall be able to recognize one another in paradise or the third heaven, that is, the temporary heaven, we shall be able to recognize each other also in the eternal heaven. Didn't our Lord confirm this in Matthew 8:11 when He said, ''I say unto you, That many shall come from the east and west, and shall sit down with Abraham, and Isaac, and Jacob, in the kingdom of heaven''? Here our Lord indicates that the personalities of Abraham, Isaac, and Jacob will be fully maintained; otherwise why would He refer to them by name? Therefore we are justified in concluding that the personalities of all the redeemed will be similarly maintained.

The Present Hell (Part 1)

Although we have examined the place to which the spirits of believers go immediately at death, we have not yet examined in detail what happens to the spirits of unbelievers, the unrighteous dead. My prayer is that you who are reading this book may not be included in this group. It is not a pleasant thing for me to speak of the punishment to which the unrighteous, that is, those outside of Christ, will be subjected, but it is the truth of the Word of God that must be declared. May this truth be used of God to hasten your repentance if you are yet outside of Christ.

Many people, including the Jehovah's Witnesses, protest that it is impossible for a God of love to punish eternally those who have not repented of their sin and unbelief. However, it is incorrect to say that God sends anyone to hell. Men actually condemn and punish themselves because they refuse to accept God's invitation to escape such a dreadful fate. God has created spiritual laws just as He has made physical laws, and foreordained the consequences of obedience and disobedience to them. If He had not done so, what would have been the use of making laws at all? This would be a world of chaos instead of order and harmony.

Every man has the ability to choose according to the light he has within himself, or which comes to him from without. Therefore every man must expect to reap the consequences of his choice. God does not determine the choice, but He determines the consequence of that choice, and warns what that will be. We read in John 3:17-19: "For God sent not his Son into the world to condemn the world; but that the world through him might be saved. He that believeth on him is not condemned: but he that believeth not is condemned already, because he hath not believed in the name of the only begotten Son of God. And this is the condemnation, that light is come into the world, and men loved darkness rather than light, because their deeds were evil."

We have no right to say that God is unrighteous because He punishes the wicked. God could not violate tha law He Himself had made. His love cannot nullify His justice. The Bible also speaks of Christ's love, a love so great that it caused Him to die on the cross as a sacrifice for sinners—including you and me. But it also speaks of His wrath, mingled with deep sorrow and pity for those who do not accept the offer of His sacrifice. It is John, the preeminent disciple of love, who presents Christ as constantly begging men to escape the wrath of God through repentance. It is love's duty to warn us by a clear presentation of what awaits us if we reject it.

We must keep clearly in mind that, just as there is a temporary paradise or third heaven to which the spirits of the believing dead go, so there is also a temporary hell for the spirits of the unrighteous dead. And as there is a final eternal heaven, so there must also be a final eternal hell.

As we have seen in earlier chapters, there are several terms used in the New Testament indicative of the place or state of punishment for the unrighteous after death.

Luke 16:22, 23 speaks of *hadees,* to which the rich man went.

Matthew 23:33 uses the word *gehenna.* "Ye serpents, ye generation of vipers, how can ye escape the damnation of hell [*gehenna* in the original]?" If *gehenna* did not exist, why should Christ mention it?

II Peter 2:4 speaks of *tartaros.* "For if God spared not the angels that sinned, but cast them down to hell [*tartaros* in the original], and delivered them into chains of darkness, to be reserved unto judgment. . . ."

Christ's teaching in Luke 16:19-31 shows that *hadees* is the place to which the spirits of the unrighteous go. Further on in this study we shall see that our Lord uses the word *gehenna* and not *hadees* to designate eternal hell.

159

The word *tartaros* occurs only once in the New Testament, in II Peter 2:4. There it is not used to indicate the place to which the spirits of the unbelieving dead go, but as the place or prison where fallen angels are kept. *Tartaros,* therefore, is the prison of the fallen angels, not the place of punishment for the spirits of the unrighteous. Jude also refers to this in the 6th verse of his epistle: "And the angels which kept not their first estate, but left their own habitation, he hath reserved in everlasting chains under darkness unto the judgment of the great day."

As we saw in a previous chapter, during the Old Testament dispensation and before Christ's resurrection, all the spirits of the dead, believers and unbelievers, went to *hadees* or *sheol* (the Hebrew equivalent of the Greek word *hadees*). We saw that *hadees* was divided into two sections, one where the righteous went, called Abraham's bosom or paradise, and one where the unrighteous went, a place of torment. And these two sections were divided from each other by a great gulf, so that those who were in one place could not go to the other. This is the description our Lord gives in Luke 16:19-31.

We also saw that, since the resurrection of Christ and His ascension to heaven, the faithful ones no longer go to *hadees* but ascend to paradise or the third heaven, where the Lord Jesus Christ now dwells. A characteristic of paradise is that it is always described as being upward, while *hadees* is said to be downward. Up there are also all the righteous ones of the Old Testament because of Christ's resurrection.

However, the dwelling place of the unrighteous dead has not been changed. *Hadees* continues to be their abode, just as it was during the Old Testament dispensation. Christ's resurrection and ascension did not affect their condition. They will remain in *hadees* until the resurrection of their bodies takes place, so that they may be judged, as we are told in Revelation 20:13: "And the sea gave up the dead which were in it; and death and hell delivered up the dead which were in them: and they were judged every man according to their works."

We see, therefore, from Luke 16:19-31 and Revelation 20:13, that *hadees* is a place for the spirits of the unrighteous dead and will continue to be so until they are resurrected in order to be judged.

The Present Hell (Part 2)

A careful study of Luke 16:19-31 discloses certain basic truths about the condition of the spirits of the unrighteous after death.

We find, for instance, that, after the rich man died and was buried, he found himself in *hadees,* that is to say, his spirit immediately went there. He was conscious of what was going on within him and around him. He could recognize Abraham and Lazarus from afar because his senses were still working. He was thirsty, he felt, he spoke, he remembered. When he asked Abraham to show mercy by sending Lazarus to cool his tongue with water, he was met with a refusal. Then he asked Abraham to send Lazarus back to earth to warn his brothers lest they, too, come to this same place of torment. But this second request was refused. Abraham said that on earth they had the prophets to warn them, if they would give heed to them. It was not necessary for anyone to go from the dead to warn them.

It is noteworthy that five times in these few verses the word "torment" or its verbal equivalent is used. Therefore we must conclude that *hadees* is a place of conscious torment.

But how do the Jehovah's Witnesses try to explain this passage of Scripture so that they may find justification for their belief that there is no place of torment for the unrighteous after death? First of all, they insist that this passage does not concern an actual event, but is merely a parable. Rutherford, one of the first leaders of the Jehovah's Witnesses, gives an entirely imaginary and completely unacceptable interpretation of this passage. In one of his books he uses nine pages to explain it. No logical mind, however, would accept such explanations, which are in brief as follows:

He believes the rich man of this story to be representative of the nation of Israel, and Lazarus representative of the Gentiles or other nations. He tells us that the drop of water stands for the very small portion of truth that could have refreshed the Jews in their despair. It is a mystery on what Rutherford bases such conclusions.

In the first place, our Lord did not refer to Luke 16:19-31 as a parable, although in many other instances when He was speaking in parables He said so. On the contrary, here we read, "There was a certain rich man . . . and there was a certain beggar named Lazarus" (verses 19 and 20). Even the name of one of the characters is mentioned, although this was not common to the other parables. But even if this story were a parable, does that change the truth of its teachings? A parable is an example or illustration whose purpose is to make clear a difficult or mysterious truth. There is no doubt that the truth the Lord wanted to teach here is the state of man after death, both of the believer and the unbeliever, the righteous and the wicked. It indicates that both are conscious; they think, they speak, they hear, they see, they feel, they remember, they recognize each other.

We have already seen that when the righteous die their spirits go to paradise or the third heaven, there to wait for the day of resurrection, when they shall receive their glorified bodies. Then they will enter the final heaven, to dwell with the Lord forever.

Something similar—yet sadly different—will happen to the unrighteous dead. Their spirits are now in *hadees,* but they will not always remain there. A thousand years after the resurrection of the righteous, the second resurrection will take place. Then the bodies of the unrighteous will be resurrected for judgment, condemnation, and consignment to the eternal hell.

What will their bodies be like? Scripture tells us nothing concerning this. But it is only logical to deduce that they will not be similar to the bodies of the saints, which Scripture describes as glorious, strong, spiritual, having the characteristics of Christ's resurrected body. We must remember that the unrighteous do not possess the gift of eternal life, but simply unending existence. We do not believe, therefore, that the bodies they receive will be "immortal," because "immortality" is a gift of God to the righteous during the first resurrection. Immortality means liberation from the corruptibility that causes pain and torment. We could logically say that the bodies of believers will be clothed in immortality, so that they will be enjoying eternal bliss, while the bodies of unbelievers will be clothed in mortality, so that they will be subject to pain and torment. It is impossible to think that God would give the same glorious characteristics to the bodies of unbelievers as He will give to believers.

In I Corinthians 15:37, 38 the Apostle Paul tells us something very significant concerning the resurrection. "And that which thou sowest, thou sowest not that body that shall be, but bare grain, it may chance of wheat, or of some other grain: but God giveth it a body as it hath pleased him, and to every seed his own body." In other words, during the resurrection the general law of sowing and reaping will be in effect. The righteous will reap the body commensurate with the seed of a righteous life, that is, one that was lived through faith in Christ for salvation and was therefore clothed in His righteousness. But those who sow the seed of a weak and corrupt nature, who die

165

without the life of Christ, cannot be resurrected with a body like that of the risen Christ. We believe, therefore, that the bodies of believers when they are raised will be "immortal," but the bodies of unbelievers will be "mortal."

When the spirits of the unbelievers now in *hadees* join their mortal bodies in the second resurrection, then will take place what the Bible calls the judgment of the great white throne. The Apostle Peter speaks of "the day of judgment and perdition of ungodly men" (II Peter 3:7). And we have seen in Revelation 20:13 that "death and hell [*hadees*] delivered up the dead which were in them: and they were judged every man according to their works." In Revelation 20:11 we read of "a great white throne," from which the unbelievers will be judged. Who will sit on this throne to act as judge? Verse 12 tells us that it will not be Christ but God the Father: "And I saw the dead, small and great, stand before God."

Today we have a unique Mediator between God and men, the Lord Jesus Christ (I Timothy 2:5). But on the day when unbelievers are judged, there will be no such Mediator. There will be no further opportunity for repentance. That day was closed at their death. Now the books in which the works of unbelievers are written will be opened, even as the books containing the works of the believers will have been opened before the judgment seat of Christ.

Before the great white throne there will be

no selection between the saved and the unsaved, because only the unsaved will appear, and each one will be judged according to his works. Nobody whose name is written in the Book of Life will appear before that tribunal.

Here are some verses that speak of the Book of Life:

Philippians 4:3: "And I intreat thee also, true yokefellow, help those women which laboured with me in the gospel, with Clement also, and with other my fellowlabourers, whose names are in the book of life."

Luke 10:20: "Notwithstanding in this rejoice not, that the spirits are subject unto you; but rather rejoice, because your names are written in heaven."

Hebrews 12:23: "To the general assembly and church of the firstborn, which are written in heaven, and to God the Judge of all, and to the spirits of just men made perfect."

Revelation 20:15: "And whosoever was not found written in the book of life was cast into the lake of fire."

Revelation 21:27: "And there shall in no wise enter into it any thing that defileth, neither whatsoever worketh abomination, or maketh a lie: but they which are written in the Lamb's book of life."

Thus the unrighteous will be judged out of the books that contain their works: "And they were judged every man according to their works"

(Revelation 20:13). It will make no difference in their lost estate whether the works of some unbelievers are not as bad as the works of others. Only those whose names were written in the Book of Life are in heaven with Christ. The judgment of unbelievers is simply to determine the degree of punishment and torment that will be meted out to them on the basis of their unrighteous works. The Word of God tells us that all unbelievers, irrespective of the degree of their unbelief and works, will be cast into the lake of fire: "And death and hell [*hadees*] were cast into the lake of fire. This is the second death" (Revelation 20:14). And verse 15 says, "And whosoever was not found written in the book of life was cast into the lake of fire."

Is your name written there? This is the most serious question you will ever be faced with in life. "Believe on the Lord Jesus Christ, and thou shalt be saved" (Acts 16:31), and immediately your name will be entered in the Book of Life. Otherwise you must face the judgment of the great white throne, from whose verdict of condemnation to eternal punishment there will be no appeal.

It is apparent that what the Word of God calls the lake of fire is the eternal hell, which for the unbeliever corresponds to the eternal heaven of the believer. "But the fearful, and unbelieving, and the abominable, and murderers, and whoremongers, and sorcerers, and idolaters, and all liars, shall have their part in the lake which burneth with fire and brimstone: which is the second death" (Revelation 21:8). The condemnation of unbelievers is general and exempts none of them. And we have seen that Scripture calls this "the second death" (Revelation 20:14).

What is meant by the second death? It is not a state of non-being, unconsciousness, or annihilation. The second death corresponds to the first death, which had to do with the corruptibility of the body; only now it has to do with the resurrected body of the unbeliever, still mortal and corruptible, in that it can suffer pain and torment forever in the lake of fire.

The Jehovah's Witnesses claim that the unbelievers will have a second chance to repent and be saved. Such a doctrine is simply the result of human imagination and wishful thinking, and not the product of divine revelation. If there is a chance for salvation after death, why does the Word of God constantly urge us to preach the Gospel to all the world and to do all in our power, including the sacrifice of life itself if need be, to spread the Kingdom of God upon earth? Why does it constantly urge us to repent and come to Christ by faith before it is too late? Why did Christ command "that repentance and remission of sins should be preached in his name among all nations, beginning at Jerusalem"? Or why did the Apostle Peter say, "The Lord is not slack concerning his promise, as some men count

169

slackness; but is longsufferring to us-ward, not willing that any should perish, but that all should come to repentance" (II Peter 3:9)?

If all men ultimately are going to be saved, why is it God's desire that all men should come to repentance right here on earth? Christ does not want anyone to be lost, but the unrighteous choose their own fate and condemnation. If it were impossible for anyone to be ultimately lost, why does Christ urge repentance and faith here and now? "I must work the works of him that sent me, while it is day," our Lord said; "the night cometh, when no man can work" (John 9:4). Whatever we do, says Christ, must be done while we are in this life. After death there is no opportunity to work or serve. How much less, then, will there be an opportunity to obtain that salvation that was neglected in this life?

The Theory of
the Restoration of
All Things, or Salvation
after Death (Part 1)

Is there a possibility of salvation after death for those who died as unrepentant sinners? This is a subject that merits careful study, for to encourage false hopes could prove fatal to many.

Why do some people promulgate such a doctrine? It arises out of their feeling that it is impossible for a God of love, mercy, and pity to punish anyone eternally. They choose to believe that ultimately He will restore all people to Himself, no matter what their beliefs and conduct may have been on earth.

We reject this theory, not only because it is indefensible in the light of human logic, but also—and primarily—because it is contrary to the Word of God. As far as logic goes, we all believe that the lawbreaker must be punished. We don't feel we are committing an injustice when we imprison a thief or any other criminal. And we believe that punishment should be commensurate with the crime committed. When it comes to God, then, why should anyone question His right to punish the one who disobeys His law, and call such a God hateful?

The punishment imposed by human justice is not supposed to bring joy to the one who imposes it, but retribution to the criminal. Punishment imposed by law does not indicate the character of the one who imposes it, but of the one who is convicted of wrongdoing. In addition, it protects the general public from further suffering at his hands. Sometimes it may by God's grace even lead to his repentance and a change for the better.

When it comes to the criminal, our main concern is the harm his activities cause to others. Upon the conviction of a lawbreaker, the one who punishes would be considered unjust if he did not carry out the sentence of the court. Wouldn't we consider God similarly unjust if He overlooked the crime of the sinner and let him go scot-free, even to rewarding him with the same eternal life and heavenly bliss He bestows upon the righteous ones?

You wouldn't feel graciously inclined toward someone who murdered a member of your family, would you? Why, then, should you expect God to be kindly inclined toward the unrepentant sinner in the last judgment? We don't believe in installing a criminal in a luxury suite in the best hotel, do we? Our human justice demands that he be locked up in jail. Why, then, should we expect God to do the opposite of what we consider just and right?

Although we know that crime should be punished, we can't always be sure that it will be. Many criminals manage to escape the punishment they deserve. On the other hand, good and honest people sometimes suffer unjustly. Ideally, our legal system is supposed to dispense unprejudiced and absolute justice, but in practice it often comes short of this ideal. Surely there ought to be an opportunity to correct inequities of punishment or reward in the world to come.

As far as God's love goes, we agree that He is no respecter of persons. He loves all His creatures equally. However, such non-prejudicial love requires that there be a time when God will mete out punishment and rewards according to the opportunities He has given every man. He sent His Son into the world to die for the redemption of all men. This does not mean that all men were then automatically redeemed by this divine act. It is necessary for each individual to respond to that act when he learns of it. "But as many as received him, to them gave he power to become the sons of God, even to them that believe on his name" (John 1:12).

If all men were to be saved, then why does Paul specify a certain period of grace by saying, "Behold, now is the accepted time; behold, now is the day of salvation" (II Corinthians 6:2)? Why was it necessary for Christ to become man and be crucified for the sins of the world, thus becoming the Saviour of men, if all men would be saved one day? The restitution of all men would do away with the necessity for Christ's redemptive act.

The condemnation for man's disobedience is general. All men are included in this category. Only those are redeemed and escape condemnation who believe in the Redeemer. If the condemnation of sinners was not to be eternal, then why such a great sacrifice by Christ?

If it were possible for those who did not repent on earth to be saved after death, they would have to repent and stop sinning on the other side of the grave. But nowhere in Scripture do we find such a possibility. Satan continues to remain Satan and end in the lake of fire, and sinners continue to possess their sinful nature, which merits eternal punishment.

Here on earth no one is forced to repent and be saved. Salvation comes to an individual when he voluntarily, in response to the operation of the Holy Spirit, accepts and receives this divine offer of forgiveness. Although God is omnipotent, He refuses to violate man's will. In spite of His desire for all men to be saved, He doesn't force them into subjection in order that His will may be accomplished. We know that He desires their salvation, as stated in I Timothy 2:4: "Who will have all men to be saved, and to come unto the knowledge of the truth." But He doesn't exercise His omnipotence in order to enforce man's salvation, for this is a matter of man's will.

Is it possible, in the world to come, for God to act diametrically opposite to the way He acted while He was here on earth? Is it possible for Him in eternity to force His salvation upon those who were unrepentant sinners on earth, and who continue to be so? It is absolutely impossible for His character to be so changeable. If God is going to change His attitude toward unrepentant sinners, canceling the punishment that is due them, what guarantee do we have that He will not do the same to believers by canceling the rewards that are due them? Hebrews 13:8 declares, "Jesus Christ [is] the same yesterday, and to day, and for ever" in His character, and since Jesus Christ is God incarnate, we see that the character of God is definitely unchangeable.

Nor can we assume that man after death ceases to have the privilege of exercising free will. He thinks, he feels, he chooses. This is why he is able to suffer if he dies unrepentant, or to rejoice if he dies as a sinner saved by grace. Sinners, even in eternity, continue to accumulate to themselves the wrath of God because of their continued sinful attitude. We find that the devil was, is, and will forever be the father of lies and deception, and his children are like him (John 8:44). The rich man could not change his state in *hadees* even though he desired to. Neither can any of the unrighteous dead. Their fate is fixed at death.

175

The Theory of the Restoration of All things, or Salvation after Death (Part 2)

When a criminal is punished by the law, he remains in prison for the duration of his sentence and is then set free, except, of course, if the punishment is death or life imprisonment. The problem we must face, if we accept the theory of eventual universal reconciliation of all men to God, is that of how the one deserving punishment can be "liberated" after death.

One of two things could happen. He must either pay in full for his sins or he must repent in order for his sentence to be remitted, either fully or partially. Take the first supposition. If the sinner could by any means within his power complete his sentence without having repented, and then go to heaven, then heaven would be full of unrepentant sinners, a manifest absurdity which the Bible precludes from beginning to end.

Besides which, if the serving of his sentence were to give the sinner the privilege of entering heaven and the joy of eternal life, we would have to conclude that man is not saved solely through receiving Christ. And conversely, if man is saved only through receiving Christ, we would have to conclude that even in *hadees,* to which the sinner goes after death, he has the opportunity to hear the Gospel, believe it, receive it, and be saved For this to take place, however, the Holy Spirit would have to be active in *hadees,* something never taught in Scripture.

While it is true that the Psalmist says, "If I ascend up into heaven, thou art there: if I make my bed in hell [*sheol*], behold, thou art there," it only indicates that God is present everywhere, but not that He gives an opportunity in *hadees* for the sinner to repent. He oversees and knows everything; otherwise He would not be God. But nowhere in the Bible do we find that the souls of sinners ascend from *hadees,* the place of torment, to paradise or heaven.

Nevertheless, those who believe in universal reconciliation cite certain verses in support of their claim. Let us examine them:

Revelation 22:2: "And the leaves of the tree were for the healing of the nations." Is the healing of the nations the salvation of all humanity? The passage in Revelation from which this verse is taken describes the rest and bliss that will prevail after the millennium of which Revelation 20:1-6 speaks. The millennium ends with a great war described in Revelation 20:7-10, caused by Satan after he is loosed. However, his end and destruction overtake him at that time.

The tree of life with its healing leaves referred to in Revelation 22:2 is a symbol of the uninterrupted health that redeemed humanity will enjoy. How many afflictions and sicknesses they suffered while on earth! These were a result of Adam's sin. Sin is spoken of in Scripture as a sickness. Satan, man's greatest enemy, was the cause of this sickness (II Corinthians 4:3, 4). Satan's aim is to keep the world in turmoil and a state of unrighteousness (II Thessalonians 2:9, 10). Thus in the New Testament we see that sickness is related to sin as well as to physical death, which is the ultimate consequence of physical sickness. And just as the leaves of certain trees may contain therapeutic elements, the leaves of the tree of life may be said to represent the healing that shall come as a result of the lifting of the curse (Revelation 22:3). This is the tree from which man in Adam was barred in the Garden of Eden when sin entered to corrupt man's nature and bring a curse upon humanity.

The nations referred to in Revelation 22:2 are the redeemed nations, and their healing is their liberation from the consequences of the curse of sin. These consequences are referred to in Revelation 21:4: "And God shall wipe away all tears from their eyes; and there shall be no more death, neither sorrow, nor crying, neither shall there be any more pain: for the former things are passed away."

There is no ground for believing that

reference is made here to the bliss of unbelievers. What is referred to is the elimination of the original Adamic curse and the full restoration of the redeemed. We could find no clearer declaration of the rejection of sinners than Revelation 21:27: "And there shall in no wise enter into it any thing that defileth, neither whatsoever worketh abomination, or maketh a lie: but they which are written in the Lamb's book of life."

We come now to another verse that people use to support their claim that God will eventually reconcile all men to Himself. It is I Peter 3:19: "By which also he went and preached unto the spirits in prison." The one who preached, of course, was Christ Himself. Verse 18 confirms this, "For Christ also hath once suffered for sins." In this verse Peter speaks clearly of the physical death of Jesus: "being put to death in the flesh." He didn't go to speak to the spirits in prison in the body He had while on earth. We are told that He was "quickened" or made alive "by the Spirit: by which also he went and preached unto the spirits in prison."

Admittedly this is a difficult verse, and there are many interpretations of it. But it is evident that Christ in the spirit, and not in the flesh, went and preached to the spirits in prison. Who were these spirits? Verse 20 tells us: "Which sometime were disobedient, when once the longsuffering of God waited in the days of Noah, while the ark was a preparing, wherein few, that is, eight souls were saved by water."

Let us remember, first of all, that "the spirits in prison" from the days when Noah was constructing the ark were not the only ones who disobeyed God down through the ages. There were many more, even as there are today, and all are the sons of disobedience. Why, then, does Peter refer specifically to those who were disobedient during the days of Noah? Apparently he wanted to show by this example that no one can claim he was unjustly condemned by God, without an opportunity, because Noah was preaching to them 120 years. But they mocked him and refused to take him seriously. (See Genesis 6:3, 11, 12, Hebrews 11:7, II Peter 2:5.)

God is a just Judge who doesn't condemn anyone without giving him an opportunity to repent. Actually man condemns himself, because he rejects his God-given opportunity to repent and accept the salvation offered by Christ. Peter cites the men who lived in Noah's day as those who most openly and flagrantly rejected their opportunity. It is not God who is to blame for their lost estate. He was longsuffering toward them. It was they themselves who were responsible, because of their disobedience. And because of this disobedience, they, and all those in whom the spirit of disobedience worked, and is now working, are condemned to imprisonment in *hadees* at death, there to await the last judgment before the great white throne.

180

There are two main interpretations of this verse. The first is that Christ, during the period between His death and resurrection, "preached" to the spirits in *hadees* who disobeyed God's warnings through Noah while the ark was being built. However, we need not conclude that "preached" means "evangelized, or exhorted to repentance." This would be contrary to the whole spirit of the Bible, which teaches that man can repent and believe in this life only. One can "preach" something else than the Gospel. The verb "preach" actually means "to declare," and a preacher can declare something other than the message of salvation in Christ. We see this in such passages as Matthew 10:27, Mark 1:45; 7:36, Revelation 5:2, etc.

We have no indication here that Christ preached salvation and redemption to the spirits who were disobedient in Noah's day. What is more likely is that Christ preached or declared to them the fact of the cross as the fulfillment of the way of escape from wrath, of which the ark of Noah was the symbol or type. They laughed at what they considered Noah's foolishness in building an ark, and as a result they perished. And mockers perish today as they scoff at the idea of the cross as the way of salvation. The disobedient of Noah's day were justly kept in prison because they set at nought the longsuffering of God who for 120 years waited for them to repent. Therefore it is logical to conclude that the preaching of Christ in *hadees* was a declaration and a confirmation of the justice of God's punishment on them. It was a demonstration that just punishment is the lot of all disobedient and unrepentant sinners.

However, if we accept the interpretation that Christ was declaring to these spirits in prison the justice of His condemnation of them, the problem is solved. We have no warrant for assuming that He was offering salvation to these spirits after death, who had rejected the opportunity given them by God during 120 years of their earthly life.

The second interpretation, which we believe to be the correct one, is as follows:

a) At the time Peter was writing his First Epistle, the spirits of those who had disobeyed God and paid no attention to His longsuffering during the days of Noah were in prison in *hadees*.

b) Christ had preached to these people through Noah, whom Peter calls "the eighth person, a preacher of righteousness" (II Peter 2:5). How did Christ preach through Noah? Peter says that the prophets of the Old Testament were "searching what, or what manner of time the Spirit of Christ which was in them did signify, when it testified beforehand the sufferings of Christ, and the glory that should follow" (I Peter 1:11). The prophets had the Spirit of Christ, and it was this Spirit that revealed to them what was going to take place in the future when Christ came. Therefore Noah, the "eighth person, a preacher of righteousness," also had the Spirit of Christ, and it was this Spirit that preached through Noah to those around him that the flood was coming and that they must repent in order to be saved. This helps us understand what is meant by "the Spirit: by which also he [Christ] went and preached unto the spirits in prison." Actually, in Greek, it is not "by" but "in" the Spirit. Christ in His Spirit went and preached to the spirits in prison "when once the longsuffering of God waited in the days of Noah." In other words, the longsuffering of God was manifested once and for all toward them in Noah's day, and it will not be manifested to them again, since they rejected it.

Christ, through His Spirit that was working in Noah, preached repentance to the people of Noah's age. The word translated "once" in I Peter 3:20 is *hapax* in Greek, which means "once and for all." This absolutely precludes the possibility that this preaching unto salvation and repentance took place in the prison of *hadees*. It was made once and for all during Noah's day.

c) As a result of men's disobedience during the 120 years of "the longsuffering of God," the people who perished as a result of the flood were existing in *hadees* as disembodied spirits at the time Peter wrote his epistle, and were suffering the just punishment of their disobedience like all other unrepentant sinners.

We believe this second interpretation is more Scriptural. It does not take I Peter 3:19 to mean that Christ preached repentance and salvation in *hadees,* but that through Noah He preached repentance to the people of that age, whose spirits were still in *hadees* at the time Peter wrote his epistle. Their unhappy condition was the result of their disobedience during the time of Noah, when the longsuffering of God was manifested to them and yet rejected.

Since this verse refers to those who disobeyed, it cannot be construed as referring to those who never had a chance to hear the Gospel, with the inference that they will have such a chance after death.

The Theory of
the Restoration of
All Things, or Salvation
after Death (Part 3)

Another somewhat problematic Scripture portion is I Peter 4:5, 6: "Who shall give account to him that is ready to judge the living and the dead. For for this cause was the gospel preached also to them that are dead, that they might be judged according to men in the flesh, but live according to God in the spirit."

In verses 3-5 of this chapter, Peter tells us that the unbelievers will give account to the just Judge. This was of comfort to the believers who at that time were being persecuted and ridiculed and is of comfort to believers now. The believer has little recourse against mockery and persecution here on earth. But the day will come, after death, when their persecutors will be judged for their behavior. But what about believers who have already died, some of whom may have suffered a martyr's death? Peter assures us that even they have heard of the coming judgment of unbelievers. "God is ready to judge the quick [living] and the dead" (I Peter 4:5).

And Peter continues in verse 6, "For for this cause was the gospel preached also to them that are dead." Observe the word "also," which means here "in addition to." The judgment of the living and the dead had not only been made known to the believers who were living at the time Peter lived, but also to the dead while they were still alive. The words "the gospel preached" is actually the word "evangelized" in Greek. It comes from the Greek *evangelizomai,* which means "to make known the good message." It is to declare the good news. The Gospel is good news, but not all good news is the Gospel. It was good news to believers who had heard it and had since died—that no unrepentant sinner would remain unpunished for his earthly injustices.

The verb *eveengelisthee,* as it occurs in I Peter 4:6, which means "told the good news," is in the second aorist tense, which refers to an act at a specific time in the past. Peter does not declare that this is happening now or that it will happen in the future. It concerns a historical past event. The believers who died had heard the good news concerning the coming judgment while they were still alive on earth, even as we hear it today. Believers in all ages need the assurance that judgment is yet to come. Note that this word "evangelize," meaning to declare good news, is also used in I Peter 1:12.

On the surface, I Peter 4:6 seems difficult, but the context helps to make it clear. The key to

186

understanding it is found in the words, "that they might be judged according to men in the flesh." The expression, "in the flesh," reveals that the Gospel was preached to men who were still in the body or in the flesh—in other words, to those who had not yet died, although when the Apostle Peter wrote they had since departed from the world.

While they were still here on earth, this sermon warned them that they were going to suffer the common judgment of death for the body. But if they accepted the Gospel they would receive spiritual life, so that when they suffered the judgment of death according to the flesh, they would continue living the life of God in their spirits that had been liberated from the flesh.

This verse tells us what was and is the purpose of preaching the Gospel, but it does not tell us whether these people responded to it by exercising faith in Christ. Only God knows this, and He will reveal it to us either at the judgment seat of Christ or during the final judgment before the great white throne.

If we were to believe that this verse meant that the good news had been preached to people who had already died and gone to *hadees,* we would be accepting a view that is contrary to all Scripture, especially as revealed in the story of the rich man and Lazarus. The phrase "in the flesh" definitely indicates that the dead of whom it speaks heard the Gospel, not after death, but during the time they were in the flesh upon earth. Thus this phrase clears up the problem, leaving no grounds for believing that the Gospel is preached to anyone after death, but is offered only to those who are "in the flesh," that is, in this earthly life. Hebrews 9:27 definitely states, "It is appointed unto men once to die, but after this the judgment." There is no further opportunity for anyone to hear the Gospel of salvation after death.

If we take the word "dead" in I Peter 4:6 to mean the spiritually dead, as it does in Ephesians 2:1 and Revelation 3:1, even then we must arrive at the same conclusion. The spiritually dead are those who, while living on earth, lack spiritual life. The Gospel is preached to them to let them know that they will be judged through physical death, as it is appointed unto men once to die, but they are being challenged to receive spiritual life now and forever through accepting the Gospel of Jesus Christ.

In verse 6, Peter speaks primarily of those who were dead when he was writing this Epistle. In the previous verse he speaks primarily about the last judgment. This will not affect the believers, those who have accepted Christ. They were made spiritually alive from the time they believed, and they continue to possess this spiritual life throughout all ages and during the last judgment.

Peter writes these words in order to

encourage those who are being afflicted and persecuted because of their faith. They have the joy, however, of possessing a life that is without end. They are not afraid of the judgment to come. It is as if he were speaking about believers who suffered martyrdom for their faith on earth, telling them that they are safe with regard to the coming judgment. This naturally encouraged these living martyrs of the faith.

It is impossible that Peter would extend the same word of encouragement to unbelievers and blasphemers of the past, present, and future. This cannot be the interpretation of this entire passage. Relentless judgment awaits such people. Christ's mercy to sinners is offered only in this life, and not after death to people who die unrepentant and have not been born again.

If an omnipotent God is going to save people after death against their will, why should He not do it while they are here on earth before their death? Why should He not give them the opportunity to enjoy fellowship with Him as soon as possible and as much as possible? If He withholds something good that He could do for men, instead of conferring it upon them as early as possible, it makes Him appear a hardhearted God who postpones goodness and its manifestations.

We know from experience, however, that sin usually hardens the heart of a man, enslaves him, and makes it more difficult as time passes on for him to exercise his free will to appropriate salvation. Sin imprisons a person. Tragically, it not only does it here on earth, but also in eternity. Therefore, repentance that does not take place in this life is impossible after death. Our destiny after death is the continuation of our present state. If we die unrepentant, we shall ever be unrepentant.

"He that is unjust, let him be unjust still: and he which is filthy, let him be filthy still: and he that is righteous, let him be righteous still: and he that is holy, let him be holy still" (Revelation 22:11). And the Lord continues: "Behold, I come quickly; and my reward is with me, to give every man according as his work shall be." As Paul warns, "Be not deceived; God is not mocked: for whatsoever a man soweth, that shall he also reap" (Galatians 6:7).

How can we logically conceive of *hadees* as a place fit for the development of virtue and holiness? It is noteworthy that the Bible gives us very clear information as to the way that leads to future eternal torment, but not a single word as to the way a man can escape from *hadees* or hell. There is not a single instance in Scripture of anyone having done this.

When the rich man in Luke 16:19-31, being in torment, asked Abraham to have pity on him and send Lazarus to dip the end of his finger in water and refresh his tongue, he was refused. How can we suppose that in the future things will be different? "Between us and you there is a

190

great gulf fixed: so that they which would pass from hence to you cannot; neither can they pass to us, that would come from thence" (Luke 16:26). There was absolutely no hope for the tormented sinful rich man. There isn't a single word in the Bible concerning the transfer of the unrighteous dead from the place of punishment in hell or *hadees* to paradise or heaven.

One wonders why those who believe in the ultimate universal reconciliation of all men to God are so anxious to spread their theory. Undoubtedly it is a comfort to sinners who have no wish to repent now. But they are doing tremendous harm to them by deluding them with the false hope that they can refuse to obey Christ's command to "Repent" now (Matthew 4:17), and be given another chance to do it hereafter. Any theory that encourages men to continue in their sin is not of God.

Can we possibly concede that men such as Nero, Herod, Hitler—all murderers of thousands of people—are one day going to be on a par with the righteous ones who became their victims? If that were so, what kind of God would He be who would permit such a thing? We could not possibly conceive of such a God. Leniency toward a Hitler or a Herod is a second crime against those whom they tortured and killed.

There is no justice at all in the belief that the only punishment of the wicked will be limited to what they suffer during their earthly lifetime. Did

Hitler really pay for his crimes against humanity? His suffering was nothing compared to the suffering he spread and the tortures he imposed. Anyone who rejects the doctrine of future eternal punishment is merely encouraging the perpertration of evil here and now. He who is not afraid of the retribution of eternity curses God and kicks others around with impunity. Even though he be the mildest-mannered of men, in essence he is denying accountability to anyone but himself; and his lack of overt wickedness still masks the sin that cursed the human race in Eden. Isn't this what Adam and Eve did when Satan persuaded them that, if they did what he suggested, in disobedience to God, they would not really die? (Genesis 3:4). It was "double-talk," of course, but it is still deceiving men today. Those who believe and propagate the theory of universal reconciliation today are not saying anything new; they are just repeating the lie of the devil in the Garden of Eden.

What the Bible Teaches about Eternal Punishment (Part 1)

Throughout the entire Bible, it is apparent that unrepentant and unbelieving sinners will be eternally punished after death. It is also apparent that believers will be eternally rewarded. However, despite this abundant evidence, some people are asking for further proof. It is as if someone basking in the warm light of the sun were asking for proof that it is shining. It is difficult to understand how those who propagate the doctrine of ultimate universal reconciliation of all men to God claim to base their teaching on the Bible.

Before we quote some of the verses they cite in support of their claim, let us look at those passages that clearly teach the opposite of this doctrine.

In Matthew 10:28, our Lord said, "Fear not them which kill the body, but are not able to kill the soul: but rather fear him which is able to destroy both soul and body in hell." And in Luke 12:5 we read, "But I will forewarn you whom ye shall fear: Fear him, which after he hath killed hath power to cast into hell [*gehenna* in the Greek text]; yea, I say unto you, Fear him." Please note that being "cast into *gehenna*" takes place after the death of the body and must therefore refer to punishment after death.

John 5:28, 29: "Marvel not at this: for the hour is coming, in the which all that are in the graves shall hear his voice, and shall come forth; they that have done good, unto the resurrection of life; and they that have done evil, unto the resurrection of damnation." What else can the resurrection of damnation mean than punishment after death?

Matthew 25:31-46: Here we have abundant indications of eternal reward and punishment. Let me just quote verses 34, 41, and 46: "Come, ye blessed of my Father, inherit the kingdom prepared for you from the foundation of the world. . . . Depart from me, ye cursed, into everlasting fire, prepared for the devil and his angels. . . . And these shall go away into everlasting punishment: but the righteous into life eternal." Here we see eternal punishment and hell as the corollary of eternal bliss and heaven.

In Matthew 13 we have several parables that teach the eternal punishment of unbelievers. Let us take the parable of the tares: "As therefore the tares are gathered and burned in the fire; so shall it be in the end of this world. The Son of man shall send forth his angels, and they shall gather out of his kingdom all things that offend, and

194

them which do iniquity; and shall cast them into a furnace of fire: there shall be wailing and gnashing of teeth. Then shall the righteous shine forth as the sun in the kingdom of their Father. Who hath ears to hear, let him hear" (Matthew 13:40-43).

In verses 47-50, we have the parable of the net that was cast into the sea. Christ concludes by saying: "So shall it be at the end of the world: the angels shall come forth, and sever the wicked from among the just, and shall cast them into the furnace of fire: there shall be wailing and gnashing of teeth." There can be no doubt that this refers to future punishment, since it is meted out by the angels at the end of the world. Undoubtedly this punishment follows the resurrection of the unbelievers.

In Mark 9:43-48 the Lord speaks clearly of the certainty and eternity of future punishment: "And if thy hand offend thee, cut it off: it is better for thee to enter into life maimed, than having two hands to go into hell, into the fire that never shall be quenched: where their worm dieth not, and the fire is not quenched" (verses 43, 44). Christ repeats this twice in verses 45-48.

We have repeatedly referred to the story of the rich man and Lazarus in Luke 16:19-31. After death, one suffers and the other rests. Not a ray of hope is given the tormented rich man in *hadees.*

All four Gospels show that Christ taught

195

the truth of eternal punishment for unbelievers as the corresponding state of eternal reward for believers. Here is what John says:

John 3:36: "He that believeth on the Son hath everlasting life: and he that believeth not the Son shall not see life; but the wrath of God abideth on him." Notice the future tense here: "shall not see life." It does not say that the time will come when the wrath of God will no longer abide on the unbeliever. Of course, it is possible for unbelievers to be partially punished here on earth, but this is not their full punishment. In reality, some unbelievers may enjoy great prosperity here in spite of their sinfulness. But this is not the end. A day of final reckoning is coming.

John 8:21: "Then said Jesus again unto them, I go my way, and ye shall seek me, and shall die in your sins." Christ makes it clear that unbelievers cannot go where He is going.

In Luke 13:24 our Lord says, "Strive to enter in at the strait gate: for many, I say unto you, will seek to enter in, and shall not be able." When is this going to be? Undoubtedly after death, because now, in this life, the door of salvation in Christ is open to all who want to enter by faith. Christ Himself said, "Him that cometh to me I will in no wise cast out" (John 6:37).

We note that the rich man in *hadees* did not ask to be transferred to paradise or the bosom of Abraham, where Lazarus was. He only sought a bit of refreshment in the midst of his torment. He also asked that Lazarus be sent to earth to warn his brothers to repent. If at some time in the future there was going to be an opportunity for the ultimate reconciliation to God of himself and all who were unrepentant on earth, including his brothers, why was he so anxious to have Lazarus sent to earth to warn his brothers before they died?

Hebrews 2:3: "How shall we escape, if we neglect so great salvation?" The implied answer is, of course, that we cannot.

Matthew 16:26: "For what is a man profited, if he shall gain the whole world, and lose his own soul?" If there is going to be an ultimate universal reconciliation, why does Christ speak of the possibility of losing one's soul?

If there really is a possibility of salvation after death, a reconciliation of the soul unto God, why does Scripture speak of the unpardonable sin? "And whosoever speaketh a word against the Son of man, it shall be forgiven him: but whosoever speaketh against the Holy Ghost, it shall not be forgiven him, neither in this world, neither in the world to come" (Matthew 12:32; also see I John 5:16).

Will Judas, who betrayed Christ, finally be saved? If so, how can we justify the words of Christ: "The Son of man goeth as it is written of him: but woe unto that man by whom the Son of man is betrayed! it had been good for that man if

197

he had not been born" (Matthew 26:24). Is it possible to imagine Judas ultimately enjoying eternal bliss along with those who sacrificed their lives for the sake of Christ?

Let us see what the Apostle Paul has to say in connection with this matter.

Romans 6:23: "For the wages of sin is death; but the gift of God is eternal life through Jesus Christ our Lord." Death here is contrasted to eternal life; therefore we conclude that this death is also eternal.

Philippians 3:18, 19: "For many walk, of whom I have told you often, and now tell you even weeping, that they are the enemies of the cross of Christ: whose end is destruction, whose God is their belly, and whose glory is in their shame, who mind earthly things." By destruction Paul does not mean physical death, for that is common to all men. He refers to something that happens only to unbelievers, their punishment, or the second death, as other Scriptures inform us.

In Romans 2:3-12, Paul gives the basic principles of the final judgment of the world. This passage leaves no doubt concerning the future punishment of unbelievers. Here are some excerpts: "And thinkest thou this, O man, that judgest them which do such things, and doest the same, that thou shalt escape the judgment of God? . . . But after thy hardness and impenitent heart treasurest up unto thyself wrath against the day of wrath and revelation of the righteous judgment of God. Who will render to every man according to his deeds: to them who by patient continuance in well doing seek for glory and honour and immortality, eternal life: but unto them that are contentious, and do not obey the truth, but obey unrighteousness, indignation and wrath, tribulation and anguish, upon every soul of man that doeth evil. . . . For there is no respect of persons with God. For as many as have sinned without law shall also perish without law: and as many as have sinned in the law shall be judged by the law.''

In writing to the Thessalonians, Paul spoke of the eternal rest of the believers and the future punishment of unbelievers in these words: ''And to you who are troubled rest with us, when the Lord Jesus shall be revealed from heaven with his mighty angels, in flaming fire taking vengeance on them that know not God, and that obey not the gospel of our Lord Jesus Christ: who shall be punished with everlasting destruction from the presence of the Lord, and from the glory of his power; when he shall come to be glorified in his saints, and to be admired in all them that believe (because our testimony among you was believed) in that day'' (II Thessalonians 1:7-10).

Hebrews 10:26, 27, 30, 31: ''For if we sin wilfully after that we have received the knowledge of the truth, there remaineth no more

199

sacrifice for sins, but a certain fearful looking for of judgment and fiery indignation, which shall devour the adversaries. . . . For we know him that hath said, Vengeance belongeth unto me, I will recompense, saith the Lord. And again, The Lord shall judge his people. It is a fearful thing to fall into the hands of the living God."

We could quote many other verses in support of the undeniable truth that eternal punishment is the lot of the unbelievers, just as eternal reward is the lot of the believers. However, we leave the reader to make up his own mind from the verses that have been quoted, which we believe to be sufficient. Search the Scriptures further and you will find ample evidence of this truth.

What the Bible
Teaches about
Eternal Punishment (Part 2)

Having studied a representative sampling of those passages in the Word of God that teach eternal punishment for unbelievers, let us now examine those verses that those who believe in the ultimate reconciliation of all men to God adduce as proof of their teaching. First let us take the Old Testament.

Psalm 22:27: "All the ends of the world shall remember and turn unto the Lord: and all the kindreds of the nations shall worship before thee."

Also Psalm 86:9: "All nations whom thou hast made shall come and worship before thee, O Lord; and shall glorify thy name."

These two verses have nothing to do with the ultimate restoration of unbelievers. They refer to the worldwide spread of the Gospel during the millennial reign of Christ. At that time Satan will be bound, and what will happen then is foretold in Revelation 20. There is not a hint in these verses that those who died in their sins will have an opportunity to repent in the future.

Another verse is Proverbs 11:31: "Behold, the righteous shall be recompensed in the earth: much more the wicked and the sinner." Those who do not believe in eternal punishment for the wicked cite this verse to show that their punishment is limited to this earth only and does not extend to their existence after death. Again, such a conclusion is completely unfounded. All that this verse is saying is that, since the righteous are afflicted on the earth, it is impossible for the wicked not to be. It says nothing about excluding the wicked from punishment after death. From many other Scriptures, as well as this one, it is to be understood that the affliction of the wicked often begins down here but does not terminate here. The reward of the righteous is completed in heaven, though in this world it is mixed with suffering. Every believer experiences this truth. Solomon is not speaking primarily of the wicked in this verse but of the righteous. If the righteous are afflicted or recompensed down here, he says, how much more the wicked. Now, if we were to use this verse as a basis for excluding the punishment of the wicked after death, we would also have to exclude the reward of the righteous after death—a conclusion that would go against the whole teaching of the Bible.

Psalm 145:9: "The Lord is good to all: and his tender mercies are over all his works." Would you believe that they cite this verse to prove that God is not going to punish anybody after death?

But if this verse is taken at face value as excluding punishment, it would have to include both the present and the future. Yet Proverbs 11:31, which we have just examined, is adduced to prove that punishment is restricted to this life on earth.

If God is going to be so kind as to forgive everybody in the future, why not do it now? Does God's mercy preclude punishing the unrepentant? In Exodus 34: 6, 7, we find His mercy quite compatible with the notion of punishment. "The Lord God, merciful and gracious, longsuffering, and abundant in goodness and truth, keeping mercy for thousands, forgiving iniquity and transgression and sin, and that will by no means clear the guilty." Here it is quite clear that, when God does not clear the guilty, it does not mean He is not merciful and gracious. In order that His mercy may be applicable to us, we must personally accept it. Christ died for the sins of all, but only those who receive Him are saved, according to John 1:12 and 3:16.

Some New Testament verses cited by the proponents of ultimate universal reconciliation are I Corinthians 15:25, 26: "For he must reign, till he hath put all enemies under his feet. The last enemy that shall be destroyed is death." These verses have nothing at all to do with the restoration of unbelievers after death. Can we say that, when we tread our enemies under our feet, that makes them happy? When Christ puts all His enemies under his feet, He is not bestowing salvation and eternal bliss on them. He is defeating them and terminating their wicked activities.

In this chapter, Paul is speaking especially of the resurrection of the bodies of believers, and their endowment with immortality and glory. He is not particularly dealing with unbelievers and the unrepentant. There are some who claim that verse 22, in which Paul says that "in Christ shall all be made alive," means that God is going to restore all men, believers and unbelievers, through the power of Christ. This does not mean God will restore and save unbelievers to eternal life. What the Apostle is saying here is that both believers and unbelievers will be resurrected through the power of Christ, a truth that is taught in many other portions of Scripture. Some will be raised to receive eternal life in heaven; others will be in the "resurrection of damnation" (John 5:29).

The fact that all the dead, both believers and unbelievers, will be resurrected so that they can account for the deeds done on earth does not mean that all will end up in heaven. "And that servant, which knew his lord's will, and prepared not himself, neither did according to his will, shall be beaten with many stripes. But he that knew not, and did commit things worthy of stripes, shall be beaten with few stripes. For unto whomsoever much is given, of him shall be much required: and to whom men have committed much, of him they will ask the more" (Luke 12:47, 48). These verses teach that not all unbelievers will receive the same punishment. There will be degrees of punishment, according to their works of unbelief and sin. But we must not confuse the resurrection of believers and unbelievers with the notion of the restoration of all to the same eternal state. That the resurrection of all does not mean the eternal bliss of all is readily seen from the words of Christ Himself in John 5:28, 29: "All that are in the graves . . . shall come forth; they that have done good, unto the resurrection of life; and they that have done evil, unto the resurrection of damnation."

Another verse is Colossians 1:20: "And having made peace through the blood of his cross, by him [Christ] to reconcile all things unto himself." We find something similar in Ephesians 1:10: "That in the dispensation of the fulness of times he might gather together in one all things in Christ, both which are in heaven, and which are on earth; even in him." Again, they cite II Corinthians 5:19: "God was in Christ, reconciling the world unto himself, not imputing their trespasses unto them; and hath committed unto us the word of reconciliation." A similar statement is found in Philippians 2:11: "And that every tongue should confess that Jesus Christ is Lord, to the glory of God the Father."

We could take each of these verses and explain them in detail, proving beyond the shadow of a doubt that they do not teach anything contrary to the clear declaration of Scripture, particularly the declaration of Christ Himself, that the wicked dead are eternally lost. To do this, however, we would have to take these verses in their general context and examine the whole chapter in which each is found, if not the entire epistles from which they are taken. We shall do this as briefly as we know how, allowing the reader to make a more extensive personal study.

First let us consider the use of the words "each," "every," and "all." In Colossians chapter 1 Paul presents Christ as the Creator of all things: "For by him were all things created . . . all things were created by him, and for him" (Col. 1:16). Also, in verse 17, we read that "by him all things consist." These verses declare the absolute sovereignty of the Lord in His creation and preservation of the world.

It is important for us to realize that the words "every one" and "all" are not always used with the sense of every human being, or every thing. The meaning depends on what things or what truths these words refer to. There may be restrictions and qualifications implied.

You will readily understand this if you look at I John 5:19: "And we know that we are of God, and the whole world lieth in wickedness." Here we have what would seem to be an all-inclusive term, "The whole world." Does John mean that every man in the world "lieth in wickedness"? Impossible, since he has just said that "We know that we are of God." John simply means that the majority of the human race then living were "in wickedness."

Or take Colossians 1:23. Paul refers here to the Gospel "which was preached to every creature which is under heaven." Now does Paul actually mean that every living soul had heard the Gospel? No, he is referring rather to the creation under heaven where the Gospel had been preached, to every man to whom the truth had been preached, and not to every living individual under heaven. Thus we see how an all-inclusive statement must be qualified and limited in its application.

Another example is found in I Corinthians 10:23, where Paul says, "All things are lawful for me." Does Paul mean by this that he can with a clear conscience disobey the entire moral law of God? Impossible. The expression "all" here must be qualified by "all that is permitted by the moral law," and Paul goes on to say that even then such liberty may not be expedient, since it might not be the best example for others. We must place the same limitation on I Corinthians 13:7, that love "believeth all things." We couldn't by any stretch of the imagination make this mean that love believes a lie and a deception.

In Colossians 1:18 Paul refers to Christ as "the head of the body, the church." The reconciliation to Him of all things, mentioned in verse 20, refers to the completion of His Church from among those on earth and in heaven. It nowhere states that Christ is going to reconcile to Himself *hadees* and those who are in it.

As far as the reconciliation of the world or the creation to Christ, such expressions do not predict the final salvation of all men after death, but rather the subjugation by the Lord of the whole creation when' He comes in glory. The world today in all its manifestations—physical, material, or natural—is in a general state of apostasy from God. The whole creation is out of harmony with its Creator. That is why we experience suffering in this world.

Paul tells us that the devil is the present prince of this world, who deceives it. The term "world" here indicates the world insofar as it is wicked. This does not mean that Satan now or ever has had or will have absolute power over creation. In Ephesians 2:2 he calls him, "The prince of the power of the air, the spirit that now worketh in the children of disobedience." Christ is not going to save the devil or the sons of disobedience; He is going to subjugate them. He brings about His peace and harmony in two ways: through mercy in those who voluntarily receive Him, and by force by putting under His feet those who reject Him. And those who have received His peace by faith will live undisturbed in eternal righteousness; while those who have rejected

Him will be punished eternally.

In I Corinthians 15:24, we read of a time "when he shall have put down all rule and all authority and power." This does not refer to a saving reconciliation but to a subjugating restoration of His order by restricting evil and punishing evildoers, thus eliminating the possibility of evil.

Throughout the entire Bible we see Christ presented as the Redeemer of all who believe, and the subjugator of all who do not believe, so that His eternal purposes may be realized and His absolute sovereignty applied. For the believers, it will be eternal joy because of their voluntary obedience; but for the unbelievers it will be involuntary subjugation, bringing sorrow and punishment.

What Is Meant by Christ's Regeneration?

In Matthew 19:28 we read: "And Jesus said unto them, Verily I say unto you, that ye which have followed me, in the regeneration when the Son of man shall sit in the throne of his glory, ye also shall sit upon twelve thrones, judging the twelve tribes of Israel."

The Greek word for "regeneration" here is *palingenesia,* while the word used in John 3:3, 7 and translated "born again" is *genneethee* and *genneetheenai anoothen* in its verbal form. *Palingenesia* is made up of the adverb *palin,* which means "anew, again," and *genneesis,* which means "birth, creation, production." Therefore it means the new production or creation. The expression *anoothen,* "from above," coupled with the verb *gennaoo,* refers to an entirely new creation which is brought about, not from beneath but from above. It concerns the entrance of man into the spiritual world of heaven.

In Matthew 19:28 the word *palingenesia,* meaning "re-creation," does not refer to the establishment of Christ's Kingdom within the human heart, a spiritual birth, but to a new creation of the state of affairs in which the unbelieving Israelites will be judged. They are not now being judged corporately. But this verse states that the apostles will act as judges with Christ, and the believers will judge similarly.

In Matthew 16:27 we read: "For the Son of man shall come in the glory of his Father with his angels; and then he shall reward every man according to his works." (See also Matthew 25:31, 32, I Corinthians 4:5, II Timothy 4:1, Jude 14, 15.) Usually in Scripture we do not find Christ sitting on a throne in glory when He is about to save somebody, but only when He is about to judge somebody. Paul says in I Corinthians 6:2, "Do ye not know that the saints shall judge the world?" (See also Psalm 91:14, Isaiah 58:14, Daniel 12:3, Habakkuk 3:19, and Luke 19:17.) And Revelation 3:21 says, "To him that overcometh will I grant to sit with me in my throne, even as I also overcame, and am set down with my Father in his throne."

This judgment of Christ in which His saints participate will bring about a new state in the world—in reality, a new creation. The devil will be toppled from his throne and Christ will be enthroned. Israel will be judged for its unbelief as a nation, corporately. The Apostle Peter clearly warned of this to the Israelites of his time in Acts 3:19-21: "Repent ye therefore, and be converted, that your sins may be blotted out, when the times of refreshing shall come from the presence of the Lord; and he shall send Jesus Christ, which before was preached unto you: whom the heaven must receive until the times of restitution of all things, which God hath spoken by the mouth of all his holy prophets since the world began."

Christ is now in heaven. He will come again to fulfill all the prophecies of the future. Israel, which is now in an apostate state, will be reconciled and restored as they recognize Christ as their Messiah. The Word of God speaks very clearly of the restoration of Israel in Isaiah 1:26; 11:12; 33:20; 40:2; 49:22; 60:10; Ezekiel 20:40; 36:8; Zechariah 1:17; 10:6, 14:11; and Malachi 3:4.

Whatever God has promised in His Word He will bring to pass. We saw this in Acts 3:21, where Peter spoke of "the times of restitution of all things, which God hath spoken by the mouth of all his holy prophets since the world began." How illogical to claim that this verse speaks of the final restitution of unbelievers to God's favor. It speaks of the fulfillment of every prophecy found in the Word of God.

God's Word tells us that, in the present state of the world, when Satan is free to act along with his emissaries, "the whole creation groaneth and travaileth in pain together until now" (Romans 8:22). Not even believers are exempt from the influence of evil, despite the fact that they are indwelt and governed by Jesus Christ. As Romans 8:23 reminds us, "Ourselves also, which have the firstfruits of the Spirit, even we ourselves groan within ourselves, waiting for the adoption, to wit, the redemption of our body." This is what Paul means by the terms reconciliation, restitution, completion, and similar expressions. "Nevertheless we, according to his promise, look for new heavens and a new earth, wherein dwelleth righteousness" (II Peter 3:13). "And I saw a new heaven and a new earth: for the first heaven and the first earth were passed away; and there was no more sea" (Revelation 21:1). Only believers expect such a heaven and such an earth.

My prayer is that those who have been taught to expect a second chance for the unbeliever after death will realize that the Word of God holds out no such hope, and that they will settle the matter of their souls' salvation here and now, rather than take any risk when it comes to their eternal destiny.

The Consequences of Believing in Ultimate Universal Salvation

Just suppose there were such a chance as the unrepentant sinner being given another opportunity to be saved after death, what would be the consequences of such a belief? The Apostle Paul on occasion brought out the consequences of supposed situations in order to point out their absurdity. The 15th chapter of I Corinthians is full of such arguments. In logic they are called *reductio ad absurdum,* the disproof of a proposition by showing an absurdity to which it leads when carried to its logical conclusion.

For instance, Paul told the philosophizing Corinthians that, if their contention that there is no resurrection from the dead were true, they would have to disregard the fact of Christ's resurrection. But how can you logically put aside a fact? A hypothesis cannot ignore or cancel a historical event. "Let's see where such a supposition leads us," Paul says in effect. "But if there be no resurrection of the dead, then is Christ not risen: and if Christ be not risen, then is our preaching vain, and your faith is also vain. Yea, and we are found false witnesses of God; because we have testified of God that he raised up Christ: whom he raised not up, if so be that the dead rise not. For if the dead rise not, then is not Christ raised: and if Christ be not raised, your faith is vain; ye are yet in your sins. Then they also which are fallen asleep in Christ are perished" (I Corinthians 15:13-18).

Let us also suppose that the preachers of the ultimate reconciliation of the wicked are correct. What happens then? What are the consequences? Such teaching encourages sinners to continue in unbelief, neither fearing God nor the result of sin. Yet the Word of God brings everyone up short with the question, "How shall we escape, if we neglect so great salvation?" (Hebrews 2:3). This is a very dangerous doctrine, costing the unrepentant more than they think. Surely God's punishment will be far greater upon those who preach such a doctrine, thus encouraging continuance in sin and unrepentance.

If we were to preach such a doctrine as salvation after death for all men, while the Bible clearly teaches the contrary, why cite the Bible as an authority at all? It would be better not to profess to believe the Bible than to cite it as proof of such an unscriptural doctrine.

Furthermore, such a doctrine does away with any concept of God's justice. Many wicked people prosper on this earth, and many righteous people suffer. Are the scales never to be balanced? Will God show no favor to those who follow Him? If He treats everybody equally in the long run, no matter how they treat Him or His commandments, we certainly could not consider Him a just God.

Our society would soon revert to a state of chaos if people knew they would never be punished for their sins. It would be a mockery to have laws without at the same time pre-fixing the penalties for disobeying them. How many people could we trust to obey the laws if they knew they would not be punished for disobeying them? How many people would tell the truth in a courtroom if they were not afraid of being penalized for perjury? Those who preach the final salvation of all, whether they died in unbelief or not, should consider the chaos into which this world would be plunged if this doctrine were to apply generally here on earth. Our sense of justice rejects it. Why should not God's sense of justice preclude it also?

If there were no future punishment, then those who die in a state of wickedness would really be better off and happier than the righteous who have renounced their own selfish wills in order to do God's will on earth, or than those who have sacrificed and suffered for Christ's service. The wicked men of Noah's day would really have had a greater reward than Noah, because they perished in the flood and escaped the difficulties and sorrows of life, and would be eternally reconciled to God. What did they lose? Nothing, since they would then have gone to heaven, or would eventually go there. Then Judas would not have done so badly when he committed suicide. He would have put an end to his torments, while those of the disciples would have continued because of persecution. Such a faith justifies and encourages not only suicide but also murder; for killing someone would literally liberate him from the troubles of earth, while liberating him to eventual eternal bliss. And the murderer himself would have nothing to lose in the end.

Such a doctrine also makes repentance and a holy life completely unnecessary. Eat, drink, and be merry, for if you die you'll have time enough then to make your peace with God. If the sinner by right can enter heaven and enjoy its privileges as much as the believer, in spite of the fact that he made no effort to prepare for it by believing in and following Christ in this life, he would really be better off than the believer. Can you imagine how full heaven would be of murderers and other criminals who never gave a thought to it here on earth? How can we accept the absurd conclusion that they are going to enjoy eternal fellowship with God as much as the purest of men? If this were true, why should anyone on earth seek to live a virtuous life? If heaven is assured to us, no matter what we do, why subject ourselves to the spiritual disciplines enjoined by the Word of God?

Such a doctrine would eliminate the necessity of religion altogether. What would be the point of worshiping God or obeying Him, if those who did not would also go to heaven? Then atheism would be as acceptable a way of life as godliness. Idolatry would be just as good as worshiping God in spirit and in truth. We wouldn't need Christ's robe of righteousness for heaven. All we would need is to die, and everything would be all right. Nobody would perish, and all would come to the same place and be saved in the end. We who proclaim the Gospel might just as well give up preaching.

What, actually, is the difference between atheism and this theory of the ultimate reconciliation of all men to God? As far as it affects men's eternal destiny, none, since even the atheist, despite his unbelief, would one day go to live with God in whom he avowedly disbelieved. In fact, this theory, if true, would be worse than atheism, because it promises not only exemption from future punishment but also eternal bliss for the unrepentant sinner. It says to the murderer, "Even if you die with the most horrible crimes to your record, don't be afraid. God is so merciful He'll open up heaven with all its glory and bliss to you in the end." How could there be greater encouragement to a life of crime and debauchery than such a belief?

For anyone to enjoy a situation, he must be psychologically prepared for it and in agreement with it. The recently bereaved person is in no mood to enjoy a party, for instance. His mental and emotional state is entirely at variance with the outward circumstances. The same thing holds true of the sinner. He is in an entirely different frame of mind from that which is in harmony with the situation prevailing in heaven. How can he enjoy heaven if all his instincts are opposed to holiness? How can a person with criminal attitudes and inclinations suddenly find himself in mental and emotional rapport with all that is taking place in heaven? How could death suddenly change his entire personality?

Consider God's dealings with the Egyptians in Moses' day. The more He exhibited His power in sending plagues, the more Pharaoh's heart was hardened. Or consider the example of the ungodly in the Book of the Revelation. When God sent plagues upon them, instead of repenting and turning to Him, they prayed that the rocks and mountains might fall upon them to hide them from Him (Revelation 6:15-17). When the hail fell upon them from heaven, instead of repenting they cursed God (Revelation 16:21). And the prophecy about Satan declares that, after he has suffered for a thousand years in the abyss, he will come out as wicked as he was before (Revelation 20:7, 8).

We conclude, therefore, that the verses

cited by those who believe in the ultimate universal reconciliation of all men, and that the subjegation of all things by Christ means the reconciliation of the wicked to God, teach no such thing. They actually refer to the recognition by all men of the power, glory, and majesty of Christ, who will subjugate the wicked and unbelieving, not as friends but as enemies.

This is actually what took place on a lesser scale while Christ was on earth when He met with people possessed by demons. The Word of God tells us that "the devils [demons] also believe and tremble" (James 2:19). Does this mean that the demons accepted Christ as their Saviour and repented? Of course not! Christ subjugated them and cast them out. (See also Mark 1:24; 3:11, Luke 4:41, Acts 19:15.)

Therefore, when Paul says in Philippians 2:10, 11, "That at the name of Jesus every knee should bow, of things in heaven, and things in earth, and things under the earth; and that every tongue should confess that Jesus Christ is Lord, to the glory of God the Father," he was not referring to a recognition of Christ as Saviour and Lord to be worshiped, but to Christ as the great Conqueror exercising His power in subjecting His enemies. (See also Revelation 5:13.)

As for Satan, God's Word says he will be punished in the lake of fire (Revelation 20:10). How can anyone possibly imagine that he and his followers will be reconciled to God?

The Eternal Hell,
Gehenna, the Lake
of Fire

Now let's examine what the Word of God teaches about eternal hell and the lake of fire, or *gehenna,* into which all the wicked shall be cast after their judgment before the great white throne of God

During this present dispensation, there is no one in this eternal hell. In Revelation 19:20 we see that the first to be cast into it will be the beast and the false prophet. The devil and his angels will be cast into it later, after a thousand years have passed (Revelation 20:10). After this, all the wicked (those who will be delivered up by *hadees,* which is the present temporary hell, and whose names are not found in the Book of Life after the judgment of the great white throne) will be cast into the lake of fire to spend eternity there (Revelation 20:12-15).

In the Old Testament, the Hebrew word for this place is Tophet (II Kings 23:10, Isaiah 30:33, Jeremiah 7:31, 32; 19:6, 11-14). The corresponding expression in New Testament Greek is *gehenna,* which occurs twelve times. Christ used the expression "lake of fire" five times to describe the eternal hell. To denote this place, He used the word *gehenna,* not *hadees.*

The Greek word *gehenna* comes from the Hebrew word *Ge-hinnom,* or the valley of Ennom, which was in the seventh part of Jerusalem. In this valley there was a hill called Tophet. During the times of Isaiah and Jeremiah, there were certain apostate parents who forced their children to pass through fires they had kindled for the worship of their god Molech (II Kings 23:10). According to Isaiah 30:33, this fire contained brimstone. Later on, this valley was used as an area in which to burn the garbage of Jerusalem. Refuse was thrown from the city wall into the valley below, where a constant fire was kept going. Some of this refuse penetrated the cracks in the stone wall, breeding all kinds of worms. And Christ chose this valley of Gehenna as a symbol of eternal hell or the lake of fire.

Our Lord often used physical symbols to illustrate metaphysical truths. In Mark 9:43-48 we read, "And if thy hand offend thee, cut it off: it is better for thee to enter into life maimed, than having two hands to go into hell [*gehenna*], into the fire that never shall be quenched." In the *gehenna* outside Jerusalem, worms continued to live in spite of the constant fires, which were never quenched. Through this illustration, our Lord taught that the unbeliever will continue a conscious existence in spite of the fact that he is in the unquenchable fire of hell.

Here are other Scripture passages in which our Lord used the word *gehenna:*

Matthew 5:22: "But I say unto you, That whosoever is angry with his brother without a cause shall be in danger of the judgment: and whosoever shall say to his brother, Raca, shall be in danger of the council: but whosoever shall say, Thou fool, shall be in danger of hell fire [*gehenna*]."

Matthew 5:29: "And if thy right eye offend thee, pluck it out, and cast it from thee: for it is profitable for thee that one of thy members should perish, and not that thy whole body should be cast into hell [*gehenna*]." (See also verse 30.)

Matthew 10:28: "And fear not them which kill the body, but are not able to kill the soul: but rather fear him which is able to destroy both soul and body in hell [*gehenna*]."

Matthew 18:9: "And if thine eye offend thee, pluck it out, and cast it from thee: it is better for thee to enter into life with one eye, rather than having two eyes to be cast into hell fire [*gehenna*]."

Matthew 23:15: "Woe unto you, scribes and Pharisees, hypocrites! for ye compass sea and land to make one proselyte, and when he is made, ye make him twofold more the child of hell [*gehenna*] than yourselves."

Matthew 23:33: "Ye serpents, ye generation of vipers, how can ye escape the damnation of hell [*gehenna*]?''

Mark 9:43: "And if thy hand offend thee, cut it off: it is better for thee to enter into life maimed, than having two hands to go into hell [*gehenna*]; yea, I say unto you, Fear him.''

We see that these verses consistently use the word *gehenna* and not *hadees,* to refer to the eternal hell. And the Bible describes it as a place in which there will be fire. Here are certain verses in which the word fire occurs:

Matthew 3:12: "But he will burn up the chaff with unquenchable fire.''

Matthew 5:22: ". . . . shall be in danger of hell [*gehenna*] fire.''

Matthew 13:42: "And shall cast them into a furnace of fire: there shall be wailing and gnashing of teeth.''

Matthew 18:8: ". . . . to be cast into everlasting fire.''

Matthew 18:9: ". . . . to be cast into hell [*gehenna*] fire.''

Matthew 25:41: ". . . . into everlasting fire, prepared for the devil and his angels.''

Mark 9:43, 45: ". . . . into the fire that never shall be quenched.''

Mark 9:44, 46, 48: ". . . . where their worm dieth not, and the fire is not quenched.''

Revelation 20:15: "And whosoever was not found written in the book of life was cast into the lake of fire.''

Revelation 21:8: ". . . . in the lake which burneth with fire and brimstone."

The question arises as to whether the use of the word fire is symbolic or literal. There is no doubt that the Bible often uses the word in a symbolic sense, as in the following verses:

Psalm 78:21: "Therefore the Lord heard this and was wroth: so a fire was kindled against Jacob, and anger also came up against Israel."

Psalm 104:4: "Who maketh his angels spirits; his ministers a flaming fire."

I Corinthians 3:13: "Every man's work shall be made manifest: for the day shall declare it, because it shall be revealed by fire; and the fire shall try every man's work of what sort it is."

Hebrews 12:29: "For our God is a consuming fire."

I Peter 1:7: "That the trial of your faith, being much more precious than of gold that perisheth, though it be tried with fire, might be found unto praise and honour and glory at the appearing of Jesus Christ."

James 3:6: "And the tongue is a fire, a world of iniquity: so is the tongue among our members, that it defileth the whole body, and setteth on fire the course of nature: and it is set on fire of hell."

(Also see Jeremiah 23:29; Zechariah 13:9, Psalm 66:10-12.)

It is evident that the word fire in these verses and many others is used in a symbolic sense as something that cleanses or burns, and as something that is horrible to face. Our Lord, therefore, in using *gehenna* and its fire as a symbol of the eternal hell, was describing something that was very real, which the people knew about, in order to make clear how terrible the destiny of the wicked was going to be. It will be one of suffering and torment. And if we consider fire in its physical manifestation so terrible, how much more terrible will be the eternal spiritual state which it symbolizes.

Let us not forget that the wicked ones in the eternal hell will be disembodied spirits, because they will experience the second death. This means that they will lose their resurrection bodies, which will corrupt away—something that will never happen to the resurrection bodies of believers. The suffering and torment of the disembodied spirits of the wicked will be equally as terrible as fire is in the material world to the material body.

What a terrible future awaits unbelievers! What can you do about it? The only thing I can tell you is what Paul told the jailer in Acts 16:31: "Believe on the Lord Jesus Christ, and thou shalt be saved." This salvation that Christ offers is not only that you may escape hell, but that you may experience abundant life here on earth. There is no more satisfying life. I hope that if you have not already done so you will appropriate it by accepting Him as your personal Saviour.

227

Further Scriptural Teaching on the State of the Wicked after Death

Punishment in eternity is described in a variety of terms in the Word of God, in addition to those used in the previous chapter. Here are some of the verses that use other terminology:

Matthew 8:12: "But the children of the kingdom shall be cast out into outer darkness: there shall be weeping and gnashing of teeth."

Matthew 13:42: "And shall cast them into a furnace of fire: there shall be wailing and gnashing of teeth."

Matthew 13:50: "And shall cast them into a furnace of fire: there shall be wailing and gnashing of teeth."

Matthew 22:13: "Then said the king to the servants, Bind him hand and foot, and take him away, and cast him into outer darkness; there shall be weeping and gnashing of teeth."

Matthew 24:51: "And shall cut him asunder, and appoint him his portion with the hypocrites: there shall be weeping and gnashing of teeth."

Matthew 25:30: "And cast ye the unprofitable servant into outer darkness: there shall be weeping and gnashing of teeth."

Luke 13:28: "There shall be weeping and gnashing of teeth, when ye shall see Abraham, and Isaac, and Jacob, and all the prophets, in the kingdom of God, and you yourselves thrust out."

In all these verses we see that the terms "outer darkness," "furnace of fire," etc., are coupled with "weeping and gnashing of teeth." There is no doubt that they refer to future punishment as decreed by God, and that such punishment is so terrible that it causes profound fear and anguish. Later on we shall consider whether this punishment is eternal or not.

Some people, however, believe that at death man is extinguished—that he ceases to exist. They tell us that this will be the fate of the unbeliever, rather than eternal punishment. There are differences of opinion among those who hold this theory. Some, for example, teach that the wicked cease to exist as soon as they die and will never live again. Others, namely the Jehovah's Witnesses, and particularly their leader, Rutherford, teach that though the wicked cease to exist at death they will be recreated and given a conscious existence again, as well as a second chance for salvation. They call this recreation the resurrection. In reality, however, it would be an entirely new creation, if man at death is completely annihilated and no longer exists.

Rutherford teaches that when the wicked are recreated they will be given a second chance to live and to receive eternal life "under better conditions." The Bible, however, teaches nothing of the sort.

According to Russell, this new opportunity for those who were annihilated to live again is the judgment; and those who refuse this second chance to receive eternal life will be cast into the lake of fire and put out of existence. Therefore the Jehovah's Witnesses actually believe in two annihilations, one immediately at death, and the other at the rejection of the second opportunity for salvation. Russell and Rutherford give to the second death in the lake of fire the meaning of complete annihilation of man's existence. The Word of God, however, teaches that the spirits of the wicked will continue to exist as conscious beings who will suffer.

We have already pointed out the error of the Jehovah's Witnesses that man at death ceases to exist as a conscious being. We have also discovered that the Bible nowhere teaches that man has a second chance after death to repent and receive Christ's salvation. We proceed now to disprove the theory that when the wicked are cast into the lake of fire they cease to exist.

In order clearly to understand what the Bible teaches, we must first determine the exact meaning of the words "destroy," "destruction," "perish," "corrupt," "corruptibility," etc.

230

Nowhere does the Bible use these words to indicate a lapse into nonexistence. Let's examine some of the verses in which these words occur:

II Thessalonians 1:9 refers to the wicked, "who shall be punished with everlasting destruction from the presence of the Lord, and from the glory of his power." The Jehovah's Witnesses claim that the word "destruction" means annihilation; and they not only misconstrue this word but also a number of similar words. However, if such words really mean complete annihilation, certain declarations of Scripture become quite ridiculous. We have only to substitute the words "annihilate" or "nonexistence" for the Scriptural terms to realize this.

Let's take some verses of Scripture in which these words are used, and see how this would work:

Psalm 78:45: "He sent divers sorts of flies among them [the Egyptians], which devoured them; and frogs, which destroyed them." Certainly the frogs did not annihilate the Egyptians; they are with us to this day. They simply caused distress to come upon them because of the destruction of their agriculture.

Job 19:10: "He hath destroyed me on every side, and I am gone: and mine hope hath he removed like a tree." These words were spoken by Job. If the word "destroyed" meant annihilated, how was Job able to speak them, or to live to write them down? In fact, in the American

Standard Version, this word is translated "broken down," and could not possibly refer to annihilation.

Job 21:17: "How oft is the candle of the wicked put out! and how oft cometh their destruction upon them! God distributeth sorrows in his anger." If destruction means annihilation, how can it happen to the same man many times?

Isaiah 34:2: "For the indignation of the Lord is upon all nations, and his fury upon all their armies: he hath utterly destroyed them, he hath delivered them to slaughter." If destroyed means annihilated, how is it that these nations continue to exist?

In Hebrews 2:14 we read that Christ came to destroy the devil: "That through death he might destroy him that had the power of death, that is, the devil." But if destroy means to annihilate, did Christ really extinguish the devil? Of course not. He lives and reigns until his final subjegation in the lake of fire, where he will continue in conscious torment forever. "And the devil that deceived them was cast into the lake of fire and brimstone, where the beast and the false prophet are, and shall be tormented day and night for ever and ever."

We see, therefore, that all these words that mean torment or death could under no circumstances be construed to mean annihilation, especially when they have to do with the punishment of the wicked. Therefore II Thessalonians

232

1:9, "Who shall be punished with everlasting destruction from the presence of the Lord, and from the glory of his power," cannot mean eternal annihilation or non-existence.

Those who say that man is finally eternally annihilated, if he refuses to accept a second opportunity after death to repent and be saved, claim that no one can be cast out of the presence of the Lord, since the Lord is omnipresent. Therefore, they say, to be cast out of His presence means to cease to exist. This again betrays illogical thinking, and insufficient attention to what Scripture actually states. In Genesis 4:16, for instance, we see that it is possible for someone to be cast out of the presence of the Lord and not be annihilated, or cease to exist. "And Cain went out from the presence of the Lord, and dwelt in the land of Nod, on the east of Eden." Does this mean that Cain ceased to exist? Of course not. To be away from the Lord, separated from His presence, does not mean annihilation but a lack of contact and communion with Him, no longer experiencing His favor.

Undoubtedly the presence of the Lord is felt more vividly and appears more gloriously in heaven than anywhere else. Therefore, when the Word of God speaks of anyone as being cast out of the presence of the Lord eternally, it is the same as if man were cast out of heaven, or kept out of heaven, which is God's dwelling place as well as the dwelling place of the saved. Certainly

233

it is obvious that the words we encounter in the verses just considered cannot possibly mean annihilation, extinction, or non-existence.

Another word that the Jehovah's Witnesses claim means annihilation is "perish," which occurs many times in the New Testament. Let's examine it in the light of Scripture to determine its real significance. Take that well-known verse, John 3:16, for instance: "For God so loved the world, that he gave his only begotten Son, that whosoever believeth in him should not perish, but have everlasting life." If the Jehovah's Witnesses are right, then the words "should not perish" would mean "should not cease to exist," and the term "everlasting life" should be taken to mean the opposite of annihilation, which would be physical being.

The word "perish" means to lose one's way, to be destroyed, to be rendered useless for the purpose of which one exists. We see this clearly in Matthew 9:17, which speaks of the "bottles" (actually animal skins) into which men put wine. It says, "Neither do men put new wine into old bottles: else the bottles break, and the wine runneth out, and the bottles perish: but they put new wine into new bottles, and both are preserved." What does the word "perish" mean here—that the wineskins will cease to exist? No—it simply means that they will split open and no longer be able to serve the purpose for which they were made, to hold wine. In Mark 2:22 we find the same word in a similar context.

Here is another example to prove that the word "perish" does not mean annihilation or non-existence. In the parable of the prodigal son, when the prodigal came to himself he said, "How many hired servants of my father's have bread enough and to spare, and I perish with hunger!" It is obvious that the word "perish" here does not mean "cease to exist" but simply "suffer from hunger."

In II Peter 3:6 we read, "Whereby the world that then was, being overflowed with water, perished." But did the earth cease to exist as a result of the flood? Of course not; it continues to this day.

In Hebrews 1:10, 11 we are told that the heavens and the earth "shall perish," but the Lord remains. Does this mean that the heavens and the earth shall cease to exist? In the verse immediately following we have an explanation of the word "perish": "And as a vesture shalt thou fold them up, and they shall be changed: but thou art the same, and thy years shall not fail." Actually, then, the meaning of the word "perish" here is to change or get old.

In general, then, we conclude that the word "perish" does not signify annihilation or non-existence.

Now consider the word "lost." Our Lord said in Matthew 10:6, "But go rather to the lost sheep of the house of Israel." He refers to the

Jews as "lost sheep." Does He mean by this sheep that did not exist? We could hardly assume that Christ would tell His disciples to go to people who did not exist. The Jews were in a state of having lost their way, even as the prodigal son had done in Luke 15:24. Theirs was a condition of estrangement from God, just as the prodigal son's was a condition of estrangement from his father and his father's house. They were far away from the place they should be.

It is a well-known scientific fact that nothing is actually annihilated, but that everything changes. When we speak of a house that has been destroyed by fire, what do we actually mean? The fact is, the building has ceased to exist as a house, but the fire did not actually annihilate the elements from which it was made but changed them into other forms. It turned the wood to coal, carbon dioxide, etc.

God has made everything in such a way that it cannot be annihilated. Why should He single out His highest creation, man, for annihilation? Such words as "destroy," "perish," "corrupt," generally mean to change from their present form or being, rather than to suffer annihilation.

Also the expression "to bring to naught, to cancel" (in Greek *katargeoo*) also means to render unable to accomplish its purpose. That's how the word is used in Romans 3:3: "For what if some did not believe? shall their unbelief make the faith of God without effect?" In Greek what is translated "make without effect" is *katargeesei.* It does not mean to cause to cease to exist. Here in Romans 3:3 it does not mean the annihilation of faith, but rather its inability to accomplish its purpose.

We conclude, then, that all the words we have discussed, and others related to them, when used in connection with eternal punishment, mean the torment and punishment of the wicked, but never their annihilation.

The theory of eternal annihilation would contradict the teaching of Scripture that there are degrees of punishment in hell. In Luke 12:47, 48 our Lord refers to some who will "be beaten with many stripes" and others who will "be beaten with few stripes." And in Romans 2:6 we read that God will render to every man "according to his deeds." We are told the same thing in Revelation 20:13: "And they were judged every man according to their works." If judgment means annihilation, as the Jehovah's Witnesses claim, then we could only conceive of it as being uniform, which is not as it is presented in the Word of God.

Will the Wicked
Suffer Eternally?

How readily some people accept the doctrine of eternal reward in an eternal heaven, but balk at the doctrine of eternal punishment for the wicked. Yet one is the necessary corollary of the other. One state cannot be eternal and the other temporal, or the words of Scripture become meaningless. And if the punishment from which Christ's death on the cross frees us is not eternal, why did He go through such sacrifice just to liberate us from the temporary punishment for sin? He became obedient to the death of the cross to save us from eternal doom.

But only those are truly liberated who receive this work of Christ by faith. Christ is simultaneously a God of love and a God of justice. He cannot treat those who reject His sacrifice in the same way that He treats those who accept it. God has given men His revelation concerning the future of the wicked. If they deliberately ignore it, they are without excuse, and bring upon themselves the eternal consequences. Let us accept the words of Christ as true, and reject any contrary teachings of men as false. Let us believe what Christ said in Matthew 25:46: "And these shall go away into everlasting punishment: but the righteous into life eternal." Though these words refer principally to the nations, they can also be applied to individuals.

It is quite obvious in this verse that Christ referred to the state of bliss and the state of punishment as both being eternal. Exactly the same word, *aioonios,* is used in the Greek text for both states. How then can anyone claim that eternity applies only to the state of reward for the just and not to the other also, the punishment of the wicked? The substantive *aeoon* in Greek refers to a period of time, but all the lexicographers ascribe to the adjective *aioonios* the meaning of unending, rather than just continuing to exist for a certain period of time or one *aeoon. Aioonios,* "eternal," used 71 times in the New Testament, is the only word that describes something that has no end. There is not a single instance where it could possibly mean temporary, or lasting only for a period of time. If the word *aeoon* is used with the meaning of a period of time, the verse itself makes this clear, as for instance in Matthew 24:3 and 28:20, where the expression "the end of the *aeoon*" is used. In the King James Version this is translated "the end of the world," but the word for world is actually *aeoon.* Here it means the dispensation of this present period of grace.

However, when the adjective *aioonios,* "eternal," is used in relation to the metaphysical destiny of man, from the meaning of the verse and general context it is apparent that it never means temporal or restricted within a period of time.

II Corinthians 4:18 makes it clear that the meaning of *aioonios,* "eternal," is the opposite of "temporal." The Apostle Paul says "For the things which are seen are temporal; but the things which are not seen are eternal." In other words, those things we see will last only for a certain period of time. But the invisible metaphysical realities are not temporal but eternal, that is, they have no end.

Let us take one more example. In Romans 16:26 Paul calls God "eternal." "But now is made manifest, and by the scriptures of the prophets, according to the commandment of the everlasting [or eternal] God, made known to all nations for the obedience of faith." What other meaning than that of endlessness can this word everlasting or eternal have? If it had the meaning the Jehovah's Witnesses ascribe to it, then God could be considered a temporary deity, a God who lasts only for a certain period of time.

If, however, in all the verses cited, the word eternal means unending, what right does anyone have to give it the meaning of a temporary period of time?

There is, however, another term in the New

Testament that very clearly means unending. It is the expression "for ever and ever." The Greek is *eis aioonas aioonoon,* which literally means "unto the *aeons* of *aeons.*" Revelation 14:11 says, "And the smoke of their torment ascendeth up for ever and ever: and they have no rest day nor night, who worship the beast and his image, and whosoever receiveth the mark of his name."

The same expression is also used to denote the punishment of the devil in Revelation 20:10: "And the devil that deceived them was cast into the lake of fire and brimstone, where the beast and the false prophet are, and shall be tormented day and night for ever and ever."

This expression is also used in relation to the person of Christ in Revelation 1:18: "I am he that liveth, and was dead; and, behold, I am alive for ever more."

We find this expression used in relation to the existence of God in the following verses:

Revelation 4:9, 10: "And when those beasts give glory and honour and thanks to him that sat on the throne, who liveth for ever and ever, the four and twenty elders fall down before him that sat on the throne, and worship him that liveth for ever and ever."

Revelation 5:13: "Blessing, and honour, and glory, and power, be unto him that sitteth upon the throne, and unto the Lamb for ever and ever."

Revelation 10:6: "And sware by him that

liveth for ever and ever, who created heaven, and the things that therein are, and the earth, and the things that therein are, and the sea, and the things which are therein, that there should be time no longer."

Revelation 15:7: "And one of the four beasts gave unto the seven angels seven golden vials full of the wrath of God, who liveth for ever and ever."

This expression "for ever and ever" is used not only in relation to the person of God, but also in relation to the unending bliss of the faithful. In Revelation 22:5 we read, "And there shall be no night there; and they need no candle, neither light of the sun; for the Lord God giveth them light: and they shall reign for ever and ever."

It is manifestly unscriptural to declare that the life of the righteous will be unending, and the life of the wicked will have an end. "Eternal" is the metaphysical state of the righteous, and "eternal" is the metaphysical state of the unrighteous. God would be unjust if He simply rewarded eternally the one class of people who proved faithful and did not punish eternally the other class of people who proved unfaithful. Let's look at some Scripture verses that prove beyond the shadow of a doubt that the punishment of the unjust is to be unending, eternal:

II Thessalonians 1:8, 9: "In flaming fire taking vengeance on them that know not God, and that obey not the gospel of our Lord Jesus Christ:

242

who shall be punished with everlasting destruction from the presence of the Lord, and from the glory of his power."

Psalm 52:5: "God shall likewise destroy thee for ever, he shall take thee away, and pluck thee out of thy dwelling place, and root thee out of the land of the living."

Psalm 92:7: "When the wicked spring as the grass, and when all the workers of iniquity do flourish; it is that they shall be destroyed for ever."

In regard to these verses from the Psalms, you will remember that in a previous chapter we have already explained that the verb "destroy" does not mean "annihilate" or "cause to cease to exist," but simply refers to a state of estrangement from God and the inability to accomplish the purpose for which men were created.

Daniel 12:2: "And many of them that sleep in the dust of the earth shall awake, some to everlasting life, and some to shame and everlasting contempt."

Matthew 18:8: "Wherefore if thy hand or thy foot offend thee, cut them off, and cast them from thee: it is better for thee to enter into life halt or maimed, rather than having two hands or two feet to be cast into everlasting fire."

Matthew 25:41: "Then shall he say also unto them on the left hand, Depart from me, ye cursed, into everlasting fire, prepared for the devil and his angels."

Mark 3:29: "But he that shall blaspheme against the Holy Ghost hath never forgiveness, but is in danger of eternal damnation."

Mark 9:43: "And if thy hand offend thee, cut it off: it is better for thee to enter into life maimed, than having two hands to go into hell, into the fire that never shall be quenched." And our Lord goes on to explain further that this punishment is absolutely unending, saying in verse 44: "Where their worm dieth not, and the fire is not quenched." These words are repeated in verses 46 and 48.

Jude 13: "Raging waves of the sea, foaming out their own shame; wandering stars, to whom is reserved the blackness of darkness for ever."

We have proved, therefore, through all these Scriptures, that when the wicked are cast into the lake of fire, the final hell, they are not going to be annihilated, or cease to exist, or be transformed later in heaven, but their punishment and torment will last for ever and ever, that is to say, it will be without end.

Can Anyone Be Sure of Heaven?

Some people feel very sure they are going to heaven; others do not. But the Bible not only tells us we can be sure, but points out the way. The Apostle John wrote near the end of his Gospel, "And many other signs truly did Jesus in the presence of his disciples, which are not written in this book: but these are written, that ye might believe that Jesus is the Christ, the Son of God; and that believing ye might have life through his name" (John 20:30, 31).

The Lord Jesus Christ explained it to Nicodemus, a ruler of the Jews, this way: "Verily, verily, I say unto thee, Except a man be born again, he cannot see the kingdom of God" (John 3:3). The alternate translation of "born again" is "born from above." This means that spiritual rebirth can only come to man while he is here on earth. And without it he cannot get to heaven.

On another occasion Christ said to those who refused to believe in Him, "I go my way, and ye shall seek me, and shall die in your sins: whither I go, ye cannot come" (John 8:21). What He was saying was that those who die as sinners cannot go where He is, that is, heaven. And as we read Luke 16:19-31, we see that there is no opportunity for repentance after death. There was none for the rich man who went to *hadees*.

It is a fundamental teaching of the Word of God that heaven is closed to those who die unrepentant. John tells us in Revelation 22:11 that the wicked will not change their character in eternity: "He that is unjust, let him be unjust still: and he which is filthy, let him be filthy still: and he that is righteous, let him be righteous still: and he that is holy, let him be holy still." In other words, the unjust and filthy are not going to become holy after death; and the righteous and holy will not become sinful after death. What we are now, if continued in, will also continue in eternity. To enter heaven, one must be prepared for it by being born again here on earth, through repentance and receiving Christ as Saviour and Lord.

The Bible says very plainly, "Behold, now is the accepted time; behold, now is the day of salvation" (II Corinthians 6:2). "Prepare to meet thy God" (Amos 4:12). And only through coming to God through Christ can anyone be sure of heaven. Christ Himself said it in John 14:6: "I am the way, the truth, and the life: no man cometh unto the Father, but by me."

According to the Word of God, each one of

us will eventually have to give an account of himself. That's what Paul says in Romans 14:12: "So then every one of us shall give account of himself to God." What account will you give? Will you tell Him you are not a sinner? Perhaps not, in your understanding of the word. But you can't argue the point with God. His Word tells us, "The scripture hath concluded all under sin, that the promise of faith by Jesus Christ might be given to them that believe" (Galatians 3:22). There are no exceptions, "For all have sinned, and come short of the glory of God" (Romans 3:23). "For there is no man that sinneth not" (I Kings 8:46). "If we say that we have no sin, we deceive ourselves, and the truth is not in us" (I John 1:8). "If we say that we have not sinned, we make him a liar, and his word is not in us" (I John 1:10). "Wherefore, as by one man sin entered into the world, and death by sin . . . so death passed upon all men, for that all have sinned" (Romans 5:12).

The Word of God not only declares that all men are sinners, but also that no one can be saved by his own meritorious works. Good works should and do follow salvation, as its natural fruit, but they can never earn salvation for you, me, or anyone else. "Not by works of righteousness which we have done, but according to his mercy he saved us, by the washing of regeneration, and renewing of the Holy Ghost" (Titus 3:5). "For by grace are ye saved through faith;

and that not of yourselves: it is the gift of God: not of works, lest any man should boast" (Ephesians 2:8, 9). "But we are all as an unclean thing, and all our righteousnesses are as filthy rags; and we all do fade as a leaf; and our iniquities, like the wind, have taken us away" (Isaiah 64:6).

The fundamental question to ask yourself at this point is, "Have I received Christ as my personal Saviour; has He changed my life?" This radical change of a man's nature is what the Bible calls the new birth or regeneration. It is not the product of your own efforts, not a patching up of your old nature, but solely and completely the regenerating work of God, so that you are "born again, not of corruptible seed, but of incorruptible, by the word of God, which liveth and abideth for ever" (I Peter 1:23). Every man is born once, when he comes into the physical world; he is born again when, through regeneration from above, he comes into the spiritual world. He becomes a new creation as a result of God's intervention in response to man's repentance and exercise of faith in Christ to save him.

Scripture says, "If any man be in Christ, he is a new creature: old things are passed away; behold, all things are become new" (II Corinthians 5:17). "A new heart also will I give you, and a new spirit will I put within you: and I will take away the stony heart out of your flesh, and I will give you an heart of flesh" (Ezekiel 36:26). "And that ye put on the new man, which after

God is created in righteousness and true holiness" (Ephesians 4:24).

The necessity for the new birth arises out of the fact that the sin we inherited from Adam, as well as the sins we continue to commit, have spiritually killed us. The only thing that could help a dead person would be to receive life. And that is precisely what God gives to the spiritually dead through the new birth. In writing to the Ephesians, Paul said to them, "And you hath he quickened [made alive], who were dead in trespasses and sins. . . . But God, who is rich in mercy, for his great love wherewith he loved us, even when we were dead in sins, hath quickened us together with Christ, (by grace ye are saved)" (Ephesians 2:1, 4, 5). "And you, being dead in your sins and the uncircumcision of your flesh, hath he quickened together with him, having forgiven you all trespasses" (Colossians 2:13).

I Timothy 5:6 states the converse: "But she that liveth in pleasure is dead while she liveth." And it isn't just the "eat, drink, and be merry" crowd that are in this state of spiritual death, but all of humanity who have not received and been transformed by the new birth in Christ. "For all have sinned, and come short of the glory of God" (Romans 3:23). Because sin is a curse that fell upon the entire world through the sin of Adam as head of the race, death came upon all. That is why, if men are not born again, they will continue to live under the curse of sin and death.

Since this is the state of the natural man, it is only natural that he resists the offer of salvation in Christ. The Apostle Paul makes this clear in I Corinthians 2:14: "But the natural man receiveth not the things of the Spirit of God: for they are foolishness unto him: neither can he know them, because they are spiritually discerned." Paul further declares in Romans 7:18, "For I know that in me (that is, in my flesh,) dwelleth no good thing: for to will is present with me; but how to perform that which is good I find not." If a man like the Apostle Paul had to confess that about himself, surely we must admit our own inability to measure up to God's standard. "So then they that are in the flesh cannot please God" (Romans 8:8). For a man to please God, he must first be born of the Spirit of God, for "that which is born of the flesh is flesh; and that which is born of the Spirit is spirit" (John 3:6). And until man is born from above, of the Spirit, God cannot work in his heart "to will and to do of his good pleasure" (Philippians 2:13).

How to Make Sure You Are Going to Heaven

It is one thing to be told you must be born again in order to acquire salvation. It's another thing to know how to go about it. John 1:12 tells you the way: "For as many as received him [Christ], unto them gave he authority to become the children of God, to them that believe on his name." The only way you can be born again is to receive Christ into your heart by faith, believing in Him as God's Son, who died for your redemption.

Perhaps an illustration will make this a little clearer. Suppose you are a criminal. You are sentenced to death. Someone who loves you goes to the President and asks him to pardon you. He issues this pardon and you accept it. You believe you have been forgiven, and that your life has been spared. This is what happens when you receive Christ. You are sentenced to death as a result of Adam's sin and your own. Your sin merits death. But God loves you, and in the person of Jesus Christ He took your place on the cross and died instead of you—and of course not

251

for you only, but also for all who will believe in and receive Him.

Christ's atonement does not mean that all men are automatically forgiven, however. Each individual must believe for himself that Christ died for him, and receive His atoning sacrifice on the cross, in order to be saved and acquire this new life. This is what it means to receive or believe in Christ. It is purely a spiritual transaction between the Spirit of Christ and your spirit, which receives this life by faith, for without faith it is impossible for you to receive His grace. Hebrews 11:6 says, "But without faith it is impossible to please him: for he that cometh to God must believe that he is, and that he is a rewarder of them that diligently seek him."

Don't make the mistake, however, of thinking that faith is merely a mental assent; it must be a deep and living conviction in your heart, resulting in a true confidence in Christ. Mental assent will bring no real change in your nature, but true heart faith will be the beginning of a complete and radical change in all your attitudes and actions. "If thou shalt confess with thy mouth the Lord Jesus, and shalt believe in thine heart that God hath raised him from the dead, thou shalt be saved. For with the heart man believeth unto righteousness; and with the mouth confession is made unto salvation" (Romans 10:9, 10).

There is no way you can be saved without

repentance and regeneration. "And the times of this ignorance God winked at: but now commandeth all men every where to repent" (Acts 17:30). The one thing you must do in order to be assured of heaven is to say from the depths of your heart the publican's prayer: "God be merciful to me a sinner" (Luke 18:13). "Repent ye therefore, and be converted, that your sins may be blotted out, when the times of refreshing shall come from the presence of the Lord" (Acts 3:19). "If we confess our sins, he is faithful and just to forgive us our sins, and to cleanse us from all unrighteousness" (I John 1:9). "And the blood of Jesus Christ his Son cleanseth us from all sin" (I John 1:7).

Exercise this saving faith in Christ with all sincerity and you will experience the cleansing of your sins through His blood. From that moment on, Christ will live in you. You will be able to say with the Apostle Paul, "I am crucified with Christ: nevertheless I live; yet not I, but Christ liveth in me: and the life which I now live in the flesh I live by the faith of the Son of God, who loved me, and gave himself for me" (Galatians 2:20).

From the moment of your regeneration you have no need to fear death or the coming judgment, because you can have full confidence in the words cf Christ in John 5:24: "Verily, verily, I say unto you, He that heareth my word, and believeth on him that sent me, hath everlasting life, and shall not come into condemnation; but is passed from death unto life."

The most encouraging thing about Christ's salvation is that it is offered to anyone. God neither discriminates nor makes distinctions. "God is no respecter of persons" (Acts 10:34). "Whosoever shall call on the name of the Lord shall be saved" (Acts 2:21). Christ says, "Come unto me, all ye that labour and are heavy laden, and I will give you rest" (Matthew 11:28). "All that the Father giveth me shall come to me; and him that cometh to me I will in no wise cast out" (John 6:37). "Behold, I stand at the door, and knock: if any man hear my voice, and open the door, I will come in to him, and will sup with him, and he with me" (Revelation 3:20). "And the Spirit and the bride say, Come. And let him that heareth say, Come. And let him that is athirst come. And whosoever will, let him take the water of life freely" (Revelation 22:17).

How can you be absolutely sure of heaven? The only way you can have any certainty about it is to know you are saved. If you have any doubts about it, it may be that you have never been born again. The Word of God assures you that if you are saved you can know it. "He that believeth on the Son of God hath the witness in himself" (I John 5:10). You don't just think you have it, but you actually have such a witness in yourself. "The Spirit itself beareth witness with our spirit, that we are the children of God" (Romans 8:16).

There is no middle ground. Either you are saved or you are not. Christ said, "No servant can serve two masters: for either he will hate the one, and love the other; or else he will hold to the one, and despise the other. Ye cannot serve God and mammon" (Luke 16:13). He also said, "He that is not with me is against me: and he that gathereth not with me scattereth" (Luke 11:23). "Know ye not, that to whom ye yield yourselves servants to obey, his servants ye are to whom ye obey; whether of sin unto death, or of obedience unto righteousness?" (Romans 6:16). "Choose you this day whom ye will serve" (Joshua 24:15). "To day if ye will hear his voice, harden not your hearts, as in the provocation, in the day of temptation in the wilderness" (Hebrews 3:7, 8).

Be careful you do not neglect this most important matter on which your eternal life depends, the acceptance of Christ as your Saviour. "Seek ye the Lord while he may be found, call ye upon him while he is near" (Isaiah 55:6). "Whereas ye know not what shall be on the morrow. For what is your life? It is even a vapour, that appeareth for a little time, and then vanisheth away" (James 4:14). "Therefore be ye also ready: for in such an hour as ye think not the Son of man cometh" (Matthew 24:44).

With sincere faith in Christ, you can make the following prayer and be assured of your salvation: "Lord, I thank You that You love me and sent Your Son to die on the cross for me. I receive this work of redemption by faith. I want His blood to cleanse my heart; and Your Spirit, Lord, to make me a new creature in Christ. I want to begin to live in heaven from now on. Thank You for the new life that You give to me this moment. Help me always to honor You in my life."